FROM NEW HELOTS

From New Helots to New Diasporas

A Retrospective for Robin Cohen

Edited by

Nicholas Van Hear, Selina Molteno and
Oliver Bakewell

Published on behalf of the International Migration Institute,
University of Oxford, the Department of Sociology, University of Warwick
and the Max Planck Institute for the Study of Religious and Ethnic Diversity
by Oxford Publishing Services

Published by Oxford Publishing Services

Oxford Publishing Services
34 Warnborough Road
Oxford OX2 6JA

Copyright © 2016 individual authors

ISBN: 978 0 9550031 7 2 (paperback)
       978 0 9550031 9 6 (Kindle)

Printed and bound by CPI Group (UK) Ltd, Croydon, CR0 4YY

Contents

From New Helots to New Diasporas

vi

Foreword and Acknowledgements

It is a pleasant academic convention for distinguished scholars to be presented with a worthy collection of papers from their students and colleagues on their retirement or other significant event, like having reached a venerable age. We decided that, on Robin Cohen's seventieth birthday, something more cheerful and celebratory was called for, a *Robinfest*. Robin is still an active researcher and a friend and mentor to many younger scholars. The result was a more loosely framed event drawing together an assembly of Robin's old and new friends and a representative collection of colleagues from at least some of the universities at which Robin has taught. Some 50 colleagues and friends from the Caribbean, Africa, Europe, Canada and the USA gathered in Oxford in October 2014 for two days of reflection, celebration and recollection. This book, replete with photographs, is a keepsake of the occasion that we hope will be of interest to others who were not there.

We include a selection of the interventions and contributions, just a taste of the rich discussion and engagement shown by all the participants.

Acknowledgements
Nick Van Hear co-organized the *Robinfest* with Oliver Bakewell and Zoe Falk of IMI. We are grateful for the help of Sally Kingsborough, Jenny Peebles and Ingrid Locatelli of IMI, not to mention all the speakers, chairs and many fascinating interventions from the floor that made the gathering so stimulating and enjoyable. The event was kindly hosted by the

From New Helots to New Diasporas

Oxford Martin School. Professor Ian Goldin, its director, gave a warm welcome to all the delegates.

Financial support was provided by the International Migration Institute (drawing on a grant from the Oxford Martin School), the Department of Sociology at the University of Warwick and the Max Planck Institute for the Study of Religious and Ethnic Diversity at Göttingen. The conference dinner was held at Kellogg College where the college's President, Professor Jonathan Michie, provided a witty after-dinner speech.

Finally, we want to thank Jason Cohen, for his help in the production of this book.

Nicholas Van Hear, Selina Molteno and Oliver Bakewell

Contributors and Editors

Jimi Adesina is professor and holder of the DST/NRF South African Research Chair in Social Policy at the College of Graduate Studies, University of South Africa. He studied at the Universities of Ibadan and Warwick, where his doctorate was co-supervised by Robin. He has taught at the University of Ibadan, Rhodes University and University of the Western Cape in South Africa.

Oliver Bakewell is director of the International Migration Institute at the University of Oxford, directed previously by Robin Cohen. They have worked together closely for a number of years on general migration issues and on the Oxford Diasporas Programme.

Rosalind Boyd is currently an independent writer based in Montreal. She was formerly director of the Centre for Developing Area Studies, McGill University, Montreal and (founding) editor of the bilingual journal *Labour, Capital and Society/Travail, capital et société*. She and Robin met in the 1970s through Peter C. W. Gutkind when the journal and international labour studies were being established. Since then, Robin has been a contributor to, and adviser for, the journal.

Jeff Crisp worked for the United Nations High Commission for Refugees for many years and is a research associate at the Refugee Studies Centre, University of Oxford. Jeff and Robin have known each other since the 1970s and Robin wrote the preface to Jeff's first book on the Ghanaian working class.

ix

Josh DeWind is director of the Migration Program and the Dissertation Proposal Development Fellowship (DPDF) Programs at the Social Science Research Council, New York. Robin served on the Program committee and he and Robin have worked together on the numerous publications and projects.

Robert Fine is emeritus professor of sociology at the University of Warwick who has written extensively on social theory and South Africa. Robin and Robert have taught courses together, co-supervised students and co-authored work on cosmopolitanism.

Alan Gamlen is senior lecturer in the School of Geography, Victoria University of Wellington, New Zealand and a key member of the Oxford Diasporas Programme, which he, Nicolas Van Hear and Robin helped to frame. He is widely published, particularly on issues concerned with diasporic engagement.

Harry Goulbourne is emeritus professor of sociology at London South Bank University. He worked closely with Robin at Warwick University, and they co-edited *Democracy and socialism in Africa*.

Barbara Harriss-White is senior research fellow, Area Studies and emeritus professor of development studies, Oxford University. She was head of Queen Elizabeth House when Robin joined the department.

Gunvor Jónsson is department lecturer in the Department for International Development, University of Oxford. She is an anthropologist, with much of her work focused on West African migration. She and Robin have edited a 788-page reader, titled *Migration and culture*.

Lorna Levy is one of the stalwarts of the Anti-Apartheid Movement. Her book, *Radical engagements*, tells the story of her involvement with searing honesty. Lorna, her husband Leon, Robin and Selina have been friends and comrades for many years.

Paul Kennedy was, with Robin, one of the small group of graduate students at Birmingham in the 1960s working under Ken Post's guidance. They are co-authors of a textbook, titled *Global sociology*. Paul, his wife Sue, and Robin and Selina have been friends since the 1960s.

Roy May is another West Africanist emanating from the Birmingham stable. He is emeritus professor of politics at Coventry University. One of his papers with Robin is reproduced in this volume. He, his wife Pam, and Robin and Selina have remained friends for many years.

Patricia Mohammed is professor of gender and cultural Studies, University of the West Indies, St Augustine, Trinidad. She was a master's student working with Robin in 1977–79 and they have remained intermittently in touch ever since.

Selina Molteno is married to Robin. She is a copy-editor and sometime ballet dancer and political activist. She has recently published a compilation of her letters titled *Letters from an intrepid ballet dancer*.

Ali Rogers is senior tutor and official fellow at Keble College, University of Oxford. He is geographer and editor-in-chief of the journal *Global Networks*, which he co-founded with Steven Vertovec and Robin.

Olivia Sheringham is a postdoctoral research fellow in the School of Geography at Queen Mary University of London. While at Oxford, she and Robin worked on a research project together, the results of which are published in their joint book, *Encountering difference: diasporic traces, creolizing spaces.*

Nicholas Van Hear is deputy director of the Centre on Migration, Policy and Society, University of Oxford. He and Robin have worked closely together on the themes of development and diaspora and they have recently published a joint article on 'Diasporas and Conflict'.

Peter Waterman is a 'scholar-activist' working with the progressive research and educational centre at the International Institute for Research and Education in Amsterdam, among many other activities. In this book, he rather amusingly describes how he met Robin in a trade union bar in Lagos in the late 1960s.

From New Helots to New Diasporas: Opening Remarks

Nicholas Van Hear

Robin Cohen has been at the fore-front of migration and diaspora stud-ies for at least three decades, and as he passed his seventieth birthday in the summer of 2014 we thought it fitting to organize a retrospective of his work and contribution. What we nicknamed the *Robinfest* took place early in October 2014 at the Martin School in Oxford. As well as reunit-ing old friends and comrades, the day and a half event proved to be a stimulating review of the various political and intellectual themes and threads with which Robin and others present have been engaged – inter-national labour studies, African studies, the study of globalization and cosmopolitanism, migration studies, and the study of diaspora and creolization.

The event was divided into two parts: 'People, Places and Print' and 'Themes and Threads'. On the first day we reflected on Robin's work in relation to the various places where he has lived and worked – West and South Africa, the Caribbean, and the UK – and the people with whom he engaged in those places. This took the form of personal reminiscences of people and places, coupled with a look at how Robin's intellectual and political contribution shaped and was shaped by those people and places. The second day had a slightly different centre of gravity: we looked more squarely at Robin's intellectual contribution through the themes and threads that he followed and initiated. Of course, this was largely a false division, for as we all know the personal is political and the political personal – and one can say the same of the intellectual too.

Many on the first day reflected on their long association with Robin. In my case, this stretches over the best part of forty years, since I was a doctoral student at the Centre for West African Studies in Birmingham in the 1970s (where I also met my good friend and colleague Jeff Crisp). During and since that time Robin has been a mentor, colleague and friend.

One formative encounter among several for me as a doctoral student then was a seminar Robin ran in the later 1970s, I think on the sociology of migration, which counted later luminaries such as Paul Gilroy and John Solomos among its attendees. We discussed particular texts at each session, including passages from *Capital*, the *18th Brumaire* and suchlike. If I get my chronology right, this must have been towards the end of the Stuart Hall era at the Centre for Cultural Studies, for Hall moved to the Open University in 1979. Robin's seminar must have been part of a formative period for the writers of the collective work *The empire strikes back*, the influential work on race and racism in 1970s Britain written collectively by Gilroy, Solomos and others at CCS. I was not part of that milieu, but Robin's seminar arguably shaped some of this group's thinking, as it did mine.

I think he has had two kinds of influence that I see – and which others may recognize too. One has been where he has shared an idea or set of ideas, a new text, or author, or a novel strand of thinking. That is of course normal, or should be normal, but Robin's suggestions were usually texts or ideas that were out of my line of vision, ones I had not, nor was likely to have, thought of. I like to think the exchange of ideas was reciprocal, but I suspect I got a lot more than he did.

Another kind of very productive influence has been where there is a convergence of thinking – a meeting of the minds, an arrival on the same wavelength – that gives you confidence to develop an imperfectly formed idea. A small example for me was a paper by Robin entitled 'Hidden forms of labour protest', which looked at informal resistance to the labour process and capitalism more widely among various kinds of workers in Nigeria and elsewhere in Africa (a version came out later as Cohen 1980, available at http://www.roape.org/pdf/1902.pdf). Both Jeff Crisp and I were thinking along the same lines in our work on gold miners and farm workers respectively, historically in the Gold Coast and in Ghana later. This paper by Robin struck a chord with my thinking, though my approach came from a different milieu – from political engagement at this time (the 1970s) in an obscure but influential left libertarian group (of which we had many in those days). That group highlighted the importance of informal forms of workers' struggle as being more liberating than, for example, conventional trade-union activity: this notion is perhaps commonplace now, but was prescient then. Robin's approach chimed with this insight from current political practice.

Fast forwarding a decade or so to the 1990s, I was at the (then) Refugee Studies Programme in Oxford and Robin was at

Warwick, though often floating around the Oxford migration studies scene, such that it was then. We thought it would be a good idea to get migration studies people spread in and around Oxford together in what we dubbed the Odyssey Club. This turned out to be a sporadic gathering usually over dinner to chew the fat about migration. It was then that we realized that there were a significant number of scholars (a critical mass even) in and around Oxford doing migration-related work – a precursor perhaps of today's vibrant migration studies scene at Oxford. I am not saying that we started it all, but those days and that grouping in some ways prefigured what we have in Oxford today – seventy or more migration-related researchers – one of the largest concentrations of such scholarship in the world. However, that is enough boasting about our place in the rise of migration studies.

Bookending

For me, one of Robin's great intellectual strengths is his ability to weave together or navigate a path between political economy and culture, between the material and cultural, or the materialist and 'culturalist', to move between these and/or to draw productively on the tensions between them. The prize is to marry the material (in what we used to call a political economy approach) and the cultural. Or, more robustly, to 'emerge from the post-modernist nightmare', as Robin put it.

This does *not* mean that the cultural has become irrelevant, or that the material determines the cultural, but dare I say, there is a *dialectical relationship* between them – that is obvious. So, in the case for which Robin is best known, for example, diaspora figures both as a social formation and a cultural form (as Steve Vertovec put it).

We chose two of Robin's most influential works with which to 'bookend' or frame the *Robinfest* – *The new helots: migrants in the international division of labour* and *Global diasporas*.

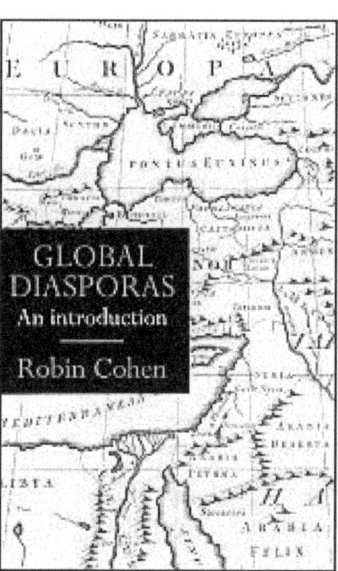

Like many others, I very much dislike the noxious metrics with which scholarship is measured these days, but it is perhaps interesting to see (crudely at any rate) how Robin's influence has risen: *The new helots*, which came out in 1987, has 520-odd Google Scholar citations, while *Global diasporas* (1997, 2nd edition 2008) dwarfs that with 3800+ citations.

Metrics aside, here I offer my thoughts on the influence of these two works, and how the two themes of the books – labour and class struggle on the one hand, and diaspora on the other – are linked. The first takes me back to a debate in the 1990s when 'diaspora studies' was just unfolding.

I remember one of our colleagues in international labour studies asking me in the mid-1990s why Robin was pursuing diaspora in his research and writing – and therefore moving away from class as the centre of gravity of his work. In this view, diaspora was an ephemeral social phenomenon, or even a phoney one. Why was Robin apparently abandoning class and pursuing this dead-end?

However, just because you do not like something does not mean that it is not worth studying – especially if it is a phenomenon of growing significance. Diasporas – in some ways like the resurgence of religion (which left-wing secularists also do not of course like) – are significant social, economic, political and cultural phenomena that need to be addressed and need explanation. Moreover, our burgeoning research in this field highlighted divisions within diaspora – not least class.

Classy diaspora

That brings me to what I think is a prominent thread in Robin's work, as with many of us perhaps, and that is the search for a vehicle or agent of (progressive) social change. Two such agents have preoccupied Robin – class and diaspora – and here my work has intersected with his.

In the 1960s and 1970s, class or classes were seen as agents of change – though there was much debate about which and how. Migrants (or at least some of them) were seen as part of the working class and they were indeed engaged in and often at the forefront of working-class struggles in the UK and elsewhere (see Linda McDowell's comparison between the Grunwick and Gate Gourmet strikes). There were also lively debates about whether or not the peasantry or 'lumpenproletariat' constituted classes, let alone classes that could act as agents of progressive change.

Of course, the wider social context – the political economy –

has since changed profoundly, as has the intellectual debate. In the face of the postmodernist blob (to subvert a Gove-ism), the argument has been that class has faded as a social force and, with that, it has also faded as a subject of study, though there has been something of a revival in recent years – witness the recent *British social class survey* and the debate it sparked. So too, largely though not wholly, has faded interest in the place of migrants in class and class in migration – though we may see a revival here too (see Davide Pero 2014; and Van Hear 2014).

As is well known, in the late 1990s and early 2000s, some scholars came to see diasporas as vehicles for change – for example, in the form of lobbying and political action in the 'host' country and/or promoting development or postwar recovery in the countries of origin. The problem with them, however, is that their solidarities are usually inward looking and exclusive – usually based on ethnicity (which was, I think, part of the 1990s' critique). In addition, as I have said and as we all know, the wider socio-political context has of course changed. People overall – and diasporas are no exception – are more atomized, individualized and entrepreneurial; they are 'neoliberal subjects' in the academic argot. Allegiances seem to be less universalist and more particularist.

In fact now the steam is perhaps beginning to go out of the idea of diasporas as vehicles of change, as Alan Gamlen, myself and others have said of the migration and development debate.

Losing the plot?
Although they remain players of global significance, when you come to look at it, the achievements are somewhat limited – diasporas may *sustain* societies through their role as purveyors

of transnational social security (remittances, relief and so forth) and this is a vital bastion against the background of neoliberal globalization's predations (Van Hear 2002, Horst 2006, Lindley 2010).

Nevertheless, the record of *changing* society – in a progressive direction at least – is mixed to say the least. Arguably, diasporas are on the whole 'small c' conservatives rather than social transformers. This is not surprising perhaps, since few diasporas are centrally motivated by the idea of social transformation – rather than shifting the balance of power among ethnic groups or other affinities.

To borrow a formulation from Marxism 'Diaspora in itself' has a somewhat shaky social formation. Diasporas are often riven with division – class, cohort, religious, ethnic, generational. 'Diaspora for itself' is at best ephemeral, in evidence during high water marks of political activity, when diasporans make common cause. Therefore, it is perhaps hard to make a case that diasporas are currently what in an earlier era some of us thought classes could be – vehicles of (progressive) change. Maybe Robin's critic in the 1990s was right after all.

The search for agents of change and the idea of changing the world for the better may now seem – and may well have been – misguided, quixotic, or quaint. However, at least some of us, like Robin, were and still are looking for some agents of change, wherever they may be found. So the call to arms is:

Abandon your Agamben!
Ditch your Derrida!
Forsake your Foucault!
Learn to speak and write *human* again – and do work that makes a difference in the world – as Robin has tried to do.

References

Cohen, R., 'Resistance and hidden forms of consciousness amongst African workers', *Review of African Political Economy*, No. 19, 1980, 'Consciousness and class', pp. 8–22. Available at www.roape.org/pdf/1902.pdf

Cohen, R., *The new helots: migrants in the international division of labour* (Gower: Aldershot, 1987).

Cohen, R., *Global diasporas: an introduction* (Abingdon: Routledge, 2008) first published 1997.

Horst, C., *Transnational nomads: how Somalis cope with refugee life in the Dadaab camps of Kenya* (Oxford: Berghahn, 2006).

Lindley, A., *The early morning phone call: Somali refugees' remittances* (New York: Berghahn Books, 2010).

Pero, D., 'Class politics and migrants: collective action among new migrant workers in Britain', *Sociology*, published online 13 March 2014, doi: 10.1177/0038038514523519

Savage, M., F. Devine, N. Cunningham, M. Taylor, L. Yaojun, J. Hjellbrekke, B. Le Roux, S. Friedman and A. Miles, 'A new model of social class: findings from the BBC's great British class experiment', *Sociology*, vol. 47, no. 2, 2013, pp. 219–50.

Van Hear, N., 'Sustaining societies under strain: remittances as a form of transnational exchange in Sri Lanka and Ghana', in K. Koser and N. Al-Ali (eds) *New approaches to migration: transnational communities and the transformation of home* (Abingdon: Routledge, 2002) pp. 202–23.

Van Hear, N., 'Reconsidering migration and class', *International Migration Review*, vol. 48, 2014. Special issue: *International migration in the 21st century: advancing the frontier of scholarship and knowledge*, vol. 48 (S1), doi: 10.1111/imre.12139.

PEOPLE, PLACES AND PRINT

1. The South African Connection

Lorna Levy

I am delighted to be here to take part in Robin's retrospective. It is a striking achievement to have produced a body of work over a lifetime that has resulted in honouring him in this way. I must confess that previously I had associated retrospectives with artists like David Hockney and Lucian Freud, but of course why should a retrospective only reflect art?

My presentation focuses on a friendship with Robin (and Selina too) that spans 50 years and shares with you some views of our South African background. I will concentrate on mine and Robin's origins because there were many similarities in our childhoods and early lives that had such a profound effect on us and shaped the people we became, giving us I believe much of our purpose and world view.

In her acceptance speech on receiving the Nobel Prize for Literature in 1991, Nadine Gordimer stressed that it was the 'place and the time' that had major implications for her existential position. I think this applies to many of us in that peculiar South African time we were growing up in the 1950s as white, privileged and segregated in our comfortable suburbs largely unaware of the peculiarly over-regulated and poverty stricken life of the majority of people around us.

Robin's South African background was comfortable, his father was a Lithuanian immigrant and a successful retail merchant, while his mother was among the first women graduates from Rhodes University.

Most middle-class South Africans from their background, and mine too, cosily accepted the status quo with a blindness about anything that disturbed the ease of that existence. That most white people accepted this as a norm and an aspect of that life, particularly those of us whose backgrounds were Jewish in an era just after the Holocaust, continues to puzzle me. The country in which we grew up was so polarized on racial grounds, yet so few whites at that time, in the 1950s and 1960s, noticed that there was a most exceptionally unfair and unequal system.

It was in the 1950s, when the Nationalist Party had taken total power in the country, that year on year the government continually rolled out a raft of new legislation to stifle any interaction of the races and to enforce what we named 'grand apartheid'.

Fortunately, in the scheme of things, there are always people of firm principle like Robin who stand for rights and wrongs, and they are the ones to be counted.

In a speech in Jerusalem in 1987, yet another South African laureate, J. M. Coetzee described South Africa as a place of 'callousness and brutality, with hungers and rages, greed and lies'. Those who opposed that status quo had to choose to take direct political action and face the consequences or quietly leave the country and not come back. In our case we adopted the first course, which resulted in an enforced period of exile in England from 1963 until we returned in 1997. Other people left when they could and did not return until the emergence of the 'New South Africa' in 1994.

Being a student at Wits [the University of the Witwatersrand in Johannesburg] was a life turning experience for many of us I think. When Robin went to Wits University as an undergraduate in 1964 he helped to run a progressive campus night school, teaching everything from literacy to 'A' levels to some 300 African workers. Wits was where a lot of white South Africans were radicalized as, at that time, it was still a first opportunity to meet students across the colour line and in his case he was to meet students who later became part of the leadership against the apartheid regime and who became prominent leaders in the new dispensation. But when he graduated with a first-class politics degree from Wits in 1964, Robin headed for London.

London in 1964 is where we all met and became friends. It was a very important place for our generation of South Africans to meet. Robin had left Johannesburg to pursue his studies and, in common with a tremendous number of others, like his brother Stan, did not intend to return to that apartheid society. Leon and I, however, belonged in that group of stateless refugees whom the Home Office allowed to remain in Britain. In one sense, the Anti-Apartheid Movement in London was just getting onto its feet and was a focal point for many of us who formed a group that I like to call the South African London Sixties Anti-Apartheid Group. And it was by the way where Selina was working at that time when she met Robin.

It was also London of the 'swinging sixties' where everything was up for discussion and society opened in a way not known before in contrast with South Africa where a right-wing

15

controlling apartheid framework of legislation was laid out year upon year tightening movement, free thought and the rights of people. It was codifying in a frightening way a separate and skewed society where the penalties for non-obedience were severe.

I believe that Robin's South African background set against the inequalities of the masses of the people around him had a profound effect and helped to shape the person he became. There were so few of us at that time who responded to those inequalities in that light so that when we met and found we shared a worldview, it forged something that just remained.

Our South African Anti-Apartheid group was significant in the scheme of that struggle because we carried the message with us wherever we went. We always tried to help bring about a change wherever we were: it remained always I believe our cause and the country never really left us wherever we were.

Over the next fifty years Robin and Selina travelled on from that first period in London to Nigeria, Trinidad, to the Midlands and finally to live in Oxford. We kept our relationship going and from time to time we actually lived in the same place. In the 1970s we both lived and left Birmingham at the same time and I remember our two daughters of the same age, Miranda and Emma, saying at the time of that move that they, aged eight I think, would like to stay behind and perhaps with their own flat so they could continue their life there.

I shall fast forward and thirty years later and at the turn of the century the Levys and Cohens were again living in the same town and it was in Cape Town. It was the period when the Cohens moved to Cape Town for three years in 2001 and Robin took up the post of Dean of Humanities at the University of Cape Town. This was a critical time for South Africa, a few years into the new dispensation and we too had only recently relocated from London to live in Cape Town. Quite clearly, Robin wanted to be part of the challenge that the new South Africa presented. Warwick University released him for four years and he hit the cutting edge of change in a university that at some levels was trying to change while at others deeply resisted the new challenges. Robin wanted to play a part in that change as it had never been far from his thoughts over the years.

The University of Cape Town's Humanities Faculty was quite a troubled place at that time as were many institutions in South Africa. They faced so many challenges and seemed unable and unwilling to implement changes that were part of the old apartheid system. UCT was a good example of the crisis that all kinds of institutions faced at that time, and 14 years later, sadly many have not been completely resolved. Humanities had become an enormous faculty comprising a range of small faculties that were hastily merged into this new faculty with portfolios like art, drama and music.

Now we have a wonderful opera school, which Robin strongly encouraged and made such a significant mark in getting going by acquiring substantial funding for it. Looking back, I always toast Robin with gratitude when I go to the opera in Cape Town that has produced astonishing stars, of whom Pretty Yende is the most famous graduate.

To return to the 1960s, it must be the period when Robin studied at the LSE and indeed later in his time at Birmingham and Warwick, the Anti-Apartheid Movement was always active on campus and needed the participation of South African activists and scholars to participate and give leadership.

There was the academic boycott which was very successful in the case of South Africa. This was spearheaded in large measure by former South African academics like Robin. There were other campaigns, which the universities in the UK organized as well, like the boycott of Barclays Bank, the marches and the rallies.

In my view, Robin belongs in that special group of South Africans, although British based for decades, who was shaped by that South African experience. He still has research links with South African universities. I am sure that South Africa is still part of him and in turn will honour his academic contributions. Although our two families have moved around so many times, changed directions and places we formed and sustained a close relationship from the 1960s in London. I think it never wavered because we remained on the left in politics wherever we were with a very well developed view of the rights and wrongs about us.

South Africa is often criticized for overplaying its exceptionalism in the world order – the idea that its apartheid past should give it some special access or dispensation. Now the argument continues: after twenty years it is a normal country with a democratic constitution and new institutions to redress the imbalances and injustices of the past and so it is no longer a special case. But that past was devastating and the legacy of racism, sexism, ethnicity, labour migration, poverty, inequality and political tyranny still haunt the new dispensation. In a perverse way, those horrific features of that South African background also inspired many South Africans, like Robin, in their research and writing.

2. If I wasn't Dr Livingstone, then he wasn't Henry Stanley

Peter Waterman[1]

Nigeria 1968

I was working for the Communist World Federation of Trade Unions in Prague and I was in Lagos to run a one-month course for its local affiliate, the NTUC. Already, before the Russians arrived in Prague to liberate me from my communism, I was wondering what I was going to do with the rest of my life.

Now the Executive De was the 'movement' restaurant. In other words, the Socialist Workers and Farmers Party had set it up with money from the communist world. It catered to movement people and office workers.

So, I was actually somewhat miffed at the appearance at the Executive De of a tallish, red-haired South African who was also clearly Jewish (it takes one to recognize one). Previously, I had considered myself a communist Dr Livingstone, boldly going where no white man had gone before. However, if I was not Dr Livingstone, then he was not Henry Stanley either.

Robin Cohen turned out, more usefully, to be a South African

---

1. I draw on my autobiography for recollections of Robin (and family) over almost a half century.

socialist doing Ph.D. research on Nigerian trade unionism, while based at the University of Ibadan. He invited me to visit him there, which I did, and he then asked me whether I would want to do a Master's degree at Birmingham University, to which he had an attachment.

It was encouraging that he was a socialist, even if he early admitted to me that when, given movement papers to sell in apartheid South Africa, his distaste for street politics would lead him to pay for them and then secretly bin them.[2]

Robin came over as a slow or relaxed, if not a diffident, person. I later discovered he was simply the most laid-back academic entrepreneur I had ever met. He not only broadened out from labour to migration and social movement studies but during the long period of left disenchantment or disorientation, in the 1980s–1990s, he held onto his political commitment – although he never made the grade as a newspaper seller. Our paths were to cross not only in Birmingham but in other places, on other occasions.

Birmingham 1969–70

My Master's course at the Centre of West African Studies was the first and only part of my tertiary education that I unreservedly enjoyed, if not entirely, well, mastered. I was able to put into it all my Prague reading and experience about Africa, and an intellect freeing itself from communism. Eight of my nine course papers were eventually published by journals like *Présence africaine*. Having never heard the expression 'peer review' I was, delighted.

---

2. Footnote added by Robin Cohen. 'Peter Waterman has got this story slightly wrong. It was the redundant copies of *Anti-Apartheid News* I was enjoined to sell on the streets of London that I disposed of in the manner described. His story is right in spirit, however. I was always much better at engaging in writing politics than in street politics.'

Then there was my new friend, Robin Cohen, who became my supervisor on a thesis about communism in the Nigerian unions. Unfortunately, this particular Birmingham degree had done away with the three-month time limit on the thesis. Even more unfortunately, I found myself a university job in Northern Nigeria, maybe 1000 km away from the union headquarters in Lagos. Robin was not entirely enchanted with what I produced after a year or two in the distant savannahs!

Montreal 1973: The New International Labour Studies
In 1972 I got myself a job I was to hold until 1998 at the Institute of Social Studies in The Hague.

While my own programme was devoting itself to 'Labour and Development', I got involved with the 'New International Labour Studies'.

Canadians hosted most of the early and crucial conferences on this theme. Although international labour studies seemed, initially, to mean 'third world labour studies', the move beyond this was made later by Robin himself. Responding to debate around the subject, he said: [3]

> I am now persuaded that we should define relevant themes in terms of (a) those issues largely concerning metropolitan capitalist countries, (b) those issues that pertain to established socialist societies, (c) those issues that are especially relevant to peripheral socialist societies, (d) those issues that pertain to peripheral capitalist countries or zones, and (e) those issues that link two or more of these groupings together, or transcend them entirely.

3. R. Cohen, 'The "new" international labour studies: a definition', *Centre for Developing-area Studies: working paper no. 27* (Quebec 1980) pp. 12–13.

According to a later contributor to this project, Ronnie Munck, I was myself giving international labour studies a distinctive political specification. Waterman, he said, was far less concerned with the academic setting and the deficiencies of area studies or traditional labour studies. He claims an explicit Marxist project and rejects the vague label of 'radical'. Where this approach scores is in its single-minded pursuit of labour internationalism, particularly through electronic communication means.

This was to lead to further collaboration with Robin.

The Hague 1978–89

During this wave of international conferences, Robin had met a couple of other researchers in the USA. In my absence, they nominated me editor of a new bulletin on the area: I bowed to the wishes of the majority. This was the *Newsletter of international labour studies* (NILS, 1978–89). It appeared more or less quarterly and it continued for a decade. During a difficult period in my professional and personal life, it also helped keep me afloat. Robin was, of course, one of the initial co-editors.

In an editorial statement in the first issue of the bulletin, I hit certain notes on the new international labour studies, additional to those already struck. One of these was to extend the address of the academic project and the bulletin to labour activists.

In the first years I got financial or practical support from Ken Post and one or two other ISS colleagues. I formed an editorial board or working group including ISS labour studies students. One was Rhoda Reddock, a former student of Robin's from Trinidad. As I moved away from the Labour Studies programme and the de-politicizing 1980s progressed, the group was reduced. Robin continued to take an interest from faraway places with strange-sounding names (Jamaica, Warwick), but was increasingly involved in migration studies. NILS ran various special issues, No. 10, 1981 being on International Labour Migration, guest-edited by Robin. The newsletter was appreciated internationally, particularly in South Africa. Many years later, my South African labour studies friend, Eddie Webster, recalled that by the late 1970s, international labour studies had 'reached the status of a new paradigm'.

Cyberspace 1990s till whenever...

Well, even before retiring from the ISS in 1998, I was exploring Cyberia and, at the same time, beginning to write my autobiography. This is entitled *From cold war communism to the global justice movement: itinerary of a long-distance internationalist*. An academic publisher accepted it. However, I then discovered that the now evidently archaic distinction between academic and vanity publishers was distinctly blurred and that I would either have to put more money than I had into this project or buy and myself publicize, sell and post a large number myself.

Having by now put my newsletter experience way behind me, I began to explore the equally ambiguous world of online publishing. Here I received detailed advice from the Oxford Family Cohen, that from Jason and Selina being followed (in their absence I seem to recall) by Robin himself. Thanks Folks! By way of thanks to him and to them, they will eventually – or even earlier than this – receive free copies of the e-book.[4] It will, unfortunately, be no freer than it will be for other hypothetical readers.

And I am hoping it won't end up, like those early anti-apartheid leaflets, in even a virtual rubbish bin.

---

4. It can be found here: http://www.into-ebooks.com/book/from_cold war_communism_to_the_global_emancipatory_movement/.

3. The Trinidad Connection: The University of the West Indies

Patricia Mohammed

I am delighted and honoured to be invited to be present here – to meet old friends and make new ones. When I requested support funds to commit the University of the West Indies St Augustine to this recollection of Robin's presence at UWI, St Augustine, from 1978 to 1980, the Dean of the Faculty of Social Science, Errol Simms, immediately agreed and willingly committed funds to it. I am thus bringing with me the weight of the UWI St Augustine homage to the time that Robin spent with us as a testament to the continued value of his work to the region. In preparation for this presentation I have also drawn on the memories of colleagues who knew Robin Cohen during his time in Trinidad and have incorporated some of their memories and tributes.

My presentation begins with a quick visual reminder to Robin of the campus as it was in the 1970s. I could lay my hands on only a few images of how it looked then and how it looks now. There are still many traces and trails of the past within the

UWI St Augustine Administration building circa 1970s

new, so although it is now an overgrown parking lot for some of us, the campus has attempted to maintain something of the pastoral beauty of its original site – the St Augustine estate, once a thriving plantation. UWI St Augustine formally opened its doors in 1960 as the result of a merger between the University College of the West Indies and the Imperial College of Tropical Agriculture. As seen in the first image, the building that currently houses a component of our administration was in fact the Imperial Tropical College of Agriculture. All of this is to say that Robin would have come to a relatively young campus then, barely twenty years old, but a space that was already rooted in a history of knowledge production, and well known for its global contribution to the science of Tropical Agriculture.

In the 1970s, a decade when many economies were in recession, Trinidad and Tobago's economy was buoyant, fed by revenues from its petroleum resources, which bolstered both the state sector and the declining agricultural sector. The 1970s' Black Power revolution, a growing disaffection by young educated as well as working-class youth who felt disenfranchized by the current government, had among its leadership students and some young faculty of the University of the West Indies. The UWI faculty of social sciences and the department of sociology that Robin had joined in 1977 from the University of Birmingham were both known for their militancy. Dr Cecilia Karsh, currently at the UWI Cave Hill campus in Barbados, reminded me that this was the tenor of the space she had joined years earlier that had coincided with Robin's appointment with the same department.

Robin's doctoral work on labour and migration in Nigeria, along with his early South African experience and later sojourn in the UK, would have well prepared him, I sincerely hope, for the kind of society he would encounter in Trinidad – its mixture of multiple races muddling their way in an era of post-colonial independence with overblown confidence and petroleum dollars. Professor Rhoda Reddock noted that, although she was not privileged to be one of Robin's students at the UWI campus (she was then working at the Cipriani Labour College nearby), she did get to know him and his family. She describes the campus that Robin joined as 'then a golden period of sociology at UWI, St Augustine. ... At that time there were stalwarts like Susan Craig, Ken Pryce and Farley Braithwaite. Sociology was at the forefront of the analysis of social challenges facing the region and globally.'

How do I come to be part of this story? I had been working on the campus at the Institute for Social and Economic Research as a research assistant and had signed up as a graduate student to do the MSc in sociology; I should remind us that this was a degree then that is equivalent to our M.Phil. degree at present. Robin had been recruited as one of our first professors in the department of sociology, which was still developing its graduate programme and was hired among other things to take us through rigorous training in theory and methodology. I recall some of the students who joined the class that year, or were there in previous years, among them Kim Johnson, Daphne Phillips, Heather Hollingsworth and Darius Figueira. All of us eventually graduated, whether in sociology or otherwise, and most have continued in some form of academia or writing. Whether this was due to Robin's influence, or to the kind of student who would choose to do graduate work at this time, is an interesting point – I would say that it was a bit of both. I think Robin had the capacity to generate enthusiasm for knowledge and spur us on to explore our individual intellectual growth rather than imposing a tailored one size fit all programme and perhaps this was exactly what the graduate programme needed at the time. For my part, he brought with him a wider understanding of a rapidly evolving global consciousness and did not confine us to the provinciality of place or space – thus already pre-figuring the global citizens of academia that we all had to become.

It was a new department and his presence in the faculty and at UWI brought multi-dimensional gains as some of his colleagues at the time recall. Brinsley Samaroo, Professor in History had this to say:

I clearly remember Robin during the late 1970s when he arrived as Professor of Sociology and soon became head of a fledgling department which he energized not only by introducing new courses but also through seminars which included staff and students from other faculties, then a rare occurrence at St Augustine. For young scholars working on diasporic studies he was particularly helpful, constantly emphasizing a global rather than a narrow geographical perspective and the need to ground empirical study on sound theory. His own writing on diasporas was a very useful guide to our research. He was always eager to learn new things about Caribbean society, looked at through his South African lens. One immediately sensed his abhorrence of apartheid when he explained the dynamics of that system to a region where the information and analysis were superficial. For that reason, his seminars on South Africa were well attended. To many of us he was friend and mentor.

Dr Susan Craig, who was a colleague of his in the Department of Sociology, observed that 'in the 1970s, when Robin Cohen joined the Sociology Department, he brought serious scholarship, a genial manner, and wide vistas.' Susan particularly remembers his generosity in assisting her with the Departmental Reader on Caribbean Sociology that she was compiling, noting that Robin read all the articles and thoughtfully ordered them into sections while Selina, his wife, also helped with translating articles from French to English.

Although Robin spent a relatively short period on the island and at UWI, he continued to maintain relationships and connections. Susan noted that when Robin was invited by the London School of Economics and Political Science to be the external examiner of her doctoral thesis in 1995, his knowledge, both of the Caribbean and of the sociology of development, was a great asset.

In my own case, Robin continued to reach out across the oceans of time and drew me into his projects. I was invited and agreed to be on the International Advisory Board of *Global Networks: The Journal of Transnational Affairs*, which Robin, Alisdair Rogers and Steven Vertovec established and edit. *Global Networks* currently ranks in the top 20 journals that deal with sociology/anthropology and globalization, no mean feat to achieve. Likewise, during my period as deputy dean from 2004 to 2007 (Graduate Studies and Research) of the Faculty of Social Sciences, I attempted to draw in the expertise of the journal and its staff to assist the faculty with developing its publication expertise and profile. Robin also invited me to present a paper at a conference on creolization that spearheaded a research project he led on creolization and diaspora in 2010 at Oxford University. Unfortunately, due to work commitments that year, I could not accept this invitation, much to my regret.

Rhoda Reddock, like Susan Craig, comments on his generosity with networks that allow for the advancement of individuals. She comments:

For me personally how well I recall my discussions with him on graduate options and my interest in the Institute of Social Studies (ISS), The Hague, which offered programmes in social development and social planning. At that time I felt the need for a more applied use of my sociological knowledge. As luck would have it, Ken Post, Professor at the ISS was visiting Robin and I was introduced, he was able to advise me on my application and the rest is history. I completed a Masters in

Development Studies at the ISS which marked the beginning of a long relationship between that institution and the UWI.

As it turned out, I completed my Ph.D. at the ISS and the project of cooperation between the Netherlands and the UWI eventually allowed for the establishment of the Institute for Gender and Development Studies of which Rhoda and I are both founding members.

The Caribbean has had a lasting impact on Robin's work. Rhoda again comments that:

His publications would always include some mention of the Caribbean or the Caribbean diaspora, which probably, due to its small size, is not often visible in many 'global' sociological texts. He also continued to engage with those troublesome concepts of 'creole' and 'creolization': concepts central to Caribbean social thought but which have begun to have a life elsewhere. This interest culminated in the 2010 volume – *The creolization reader: studies in mixed identities and cultures* co-edited with Paola Toninato, Routledge. This Caribbean-influenced reader includes Gordon Rohlehr's essay 'Calypso Reinvents Itself' addressing that quintessential Caribbean creole form – the Calypso.

How did the experience of the place and people mark Robin and how did the experience of Robin mark the place and people of the Caribbean and Trinidad in particular? I have referenced this from a range of personal recollections. I looked at the themes that are recurrent in his life's work – labour, migration, diaspora and creolization. These themes preoccupy scholars whose work and lives are enriched by experiences of displacement, multi-culturalisms and always connected to some forms of othering, in much the same way as Robin's own displacement from South Africa must have made him a constant traveller in another society. Clearly, one of the things he has successfully done is connected scholars whose shared threads of interest have created a community within the larger global fields that these themes span.

For the Caribbean, however, there is a footnote in the global landscape: Robin's seminal essay, 'Creolization and Cultural Globalization: The Soft Sounds of Fugitive Power', establishes the Caribbean as the crucial site where such ideas emerged long before it was popular to conceive of the creolized identity or the creole imaginary. In this era of new globalization, another US colleague based in New York, Aisha Khan, has also, through fully explaining the evolving landscape of culture in the Caribbean, examined and critiqued the concept of creolization. The intellectual value of this concept, born out of a new world encounter 500 years ago, clearly remains of currency in the contemporary discourses of migration, diaspora, settlement and cultural adjustment. Perhaps, this is even more so now when shifting geographies of people, involving massive urbanization in the cities of developed countries, is yet again forcing a rethinking of its explanatory significance in other contexts.

We owe a debt to scholars like Robin Cohen who lived and worked in Trinidad and found value in the minutiae of the region and in the first-hand experience of race relations that he encountered here. A South African born in a nation that was still living under apartheid, he delighted in experiencing a cohabitation of ethnic groups that presented a different model that might be emulated elsewhere. In his work, he is still invoking concepts such as creole and creolization and, with this invocation also travels the genealogy of these ideas in the work of Aimé Césaire, Frantz Fanon, Edward Braithwaite and Edouard Glissant, among others. That this is still a subject of conversation at Oxford in 2014 is an affirmation that the Caribbean continues to find a place in current global discourses and, in doing so, continuously also finds its centre.

4. Birmingham and African Studies

Roy May

I am delighted to share some thoughts with you about Robin's time in Birmingham, both at the Centre of West African Studies and the Department of Sociology.

We owe indirect thanks to Keith Panter-Brick who was due to supervise Robin's Ph.D. at LSE, but was away doing research in Nigeria. He was replaced by a visiting lecturer, Ken Post, who agreed to supervise Robin at his home base, the Centre of West African Studies (CWAS) at Birmingham.

In fact, this was a fortuitous outcome as Ken Post was far more sympathetic to Robin's ideas. Ken was teaching two MA courses – 'African Politics' and 'Politics of the Third World' – and the seminar members were Robin, Paul Kennedy (recently returned from VSO in Ethiopia), Mike Hartley Brewer (a student activist) and me (having returned from National Service in the Royal West African Frontier Force in Sierra Leone). I remember these seminars as a time of great debates and learning.

My memories are at two levels – the intellectual and the more personal. At the intellectual level, CWAS was an epicentre of great diversity and intellectual activity. One focus was the

Tuesday seminar where papers ranged from head shaping among the Yoruba to the economic history of West Africa. One paper by a rather earnest American involved him talking about the death of over half the people he had interviewed, leading to an intervention from the floor to 'stop interviewing'. On a more serious note, some of the luminaries who gave papers included Adu Boahen, Vic Allen, Tony Killick, Thomas Hodgkin, Peter Lloyd, Basil Davidson and David Apter. Apter was the proponent of a 'modernization theory', of which we were all suspicious. A memorable couplet emerged contrasting his work with that of CWAS's director, John Fage, a Cambridge historian who practised the art of rich description – 'a page of Fage is worth a chapter of Apter', somebody wrote on the CWAS notice board. It amused Apter, who saw it.

Robin contributed to this intellectual ferment with seminar papers followed by publications in the Faculty of Commerce and Social Science discussion papers, three of which I will refer to as having a significant impact. He also contributed to the many discussions with his characteristic scholarship and insight.

Publications

The first discussion paper was a very influential piece that Robin wrote with Dai Michael entitled 'The Revolutionary Potential of the Lumpenproletariat: A Sceptical View from Africa'. It addressed the contemporary debate among left-wing activists and sociologists on the search for a revolutionary class in Africa. The paper contains a sophisticated analysis of the concept and a review of case studies as diverse as the Umbandu sects, the Chinese revolution and the Kwilu Rebellion, all of which refuted the Fanonist idea that the lumpenproletariat could be turned into a revolutionary class. (In passing, they also alluded to Peter Gutkind's discussion of the Society of Loafers in Zambia.) Robin and Dai then asked the question, 'without wishing to be disrespectful, who is to storm the barricades – the beggars, the religious ascetics, the prophets, the physically disabled or the insane?' As well as upsetting some sections of the left, the paper also provoked a rather strained relationship with Dudley Seers at the Institute of Development Studies at Sussex who, with some of his colleagues, thought that phrases such as 'bourgeois social scientists' referred to them (Robin covers this dust-up on p. 120 of his book, *Contested domains*). After a number of years, a kind of reconciliation took place, with invitations to Sussex.

Another significant contribution (I hope it's not too immodest to say 'significant') was a discussion paper jointly written with me, 'The Interaction between Race and Colonialism: The Liverpool Race Riots of 1919'. It was published in *Race and Class* and is reproduced in this volume. We linked a detailed analysis of the anti-black riots in Liverpool and the impact that these had on the empire, including the Freetown riots of 1919. We also dealt with wider world events in that momentous postwar year. Robin's breadth of knowledge did much to make this the very influential piece that it has become: its ripples can be seen, for example, in Peter Fryer's *Staying power: a history of black people in Britain*, 1984.

The debates in African studies in the 1970s were moving away from the state-centric models of the 1960s and early 1970s and Robin contributed to this shift with an extremely influential article based on his work in Mauritius. This article, initially presented as a paper for the discussion series of the Faculty of Commerce and Social Science, was called 'Resistance and

Hidden Forms of Consciousness among African Workers'. Versions of the article have been republished in English at least three times and once in French. Particularly important was its publication in *Third world lives and struggle*, a course text for the Open University Third World Studies module. The paper addressed the many and various ways in which workers responded to the labour process. A particularly vivid opening quote used by Robin talks of sugar cane workers who ensured that they would work the next day by inserting a slow-burning close fuse in the cane fields, ensuring a fire. What was left of the cane had to be cut immediately, otherwise all was lost. This article (available at http://www.roape.org/pdf/1902.pdf) contributed to the later discussion on the many ways that people could escape the state and its agents. I used it much in my own work in this area.

One paper following Robin's research in St Helena provoked some interest, though Robin was somewhat surprised to see it published under another name in the *Guardian* by an unscrupulous journalist. The resulting exposé of the journalist in the pages of *Private Eye* caused us much merriment.

In conclusion, I must recall the enormous vivacity of CWAS. We had a lot of fun and talked often of a rather strange student who illegally lived in the roof! Apparently, no one in higher authority knew and we all kept the secret.

There was the annual cricket match of the Arts versus Social Sciences, a time of many happy moments. I remember sharing a couple of stands with Robin and a large number of humorous asides, we would then repair to the Gun Barrel on the Bristol Road – now gone I think. I also recall good hospitality at Robin and Selina's houses in Moor Green Lane and Cotton Lane. Here are some recollections of that time:

- When Robin offered us snoek, a South African fish that is not to everyone's taste. His mum and dad in South Africa were firmly under the impression that rationing still obtained in the UK and had sent a food parcel. He was surprised that Pam and I, having eaten this smoked fish in Liverpool just after the war, ate it with relish.

- Robin expressing his indignation when he arrived home after walking home in the rain, complaining to Selina about not having the car only to be reminded that he had taken it that morning.

- A contentious evening playing the board game 'Diplomacy'. One couple fell out dramatically when the wife colluded with Italy rather than France. The husband stormed out of the room saying, 'not only can't you keep your word but you are strategically inept and have opened a second front.'

For 48 years we have kept our friendship and debates flourishing – in Solihull, Oxford, at a pub half-way between the two and in the Vendéean discussion group when we meet in France. Robin throughout all this has provided help and advice for many colleagues and students. For me, his offer of a research fellowship at the Centre for Research in Ethnic Relations at Warwick (in 1986–7) was a pivotal moment in enabling me to shift away from heavy administration and teaching loads and forcing me back into the arena of scholarship and research.

5. Warwick University

Harry Goulbourne

My reflections on Robin's Warwick period must be generally confined to the four years (1984/5–1988/9) when he was director of the Centre for Research in Ethnic Relations (CRER). This is because, although Robin was at Warwick for some time before 1984 and remained there until 2006, he held his chair in the Department of Sociology. And, while CRER was somewhat affiliated to Sociology, as an ESRC Designated Research Centre, it operated entirely independently of the department. Robin's four years at CRER was not therefore his entire Warwick period, but they were years of opportunity to broaden the scope of the field of studying race in Britain. This was a defining period, I believe, for Robin as well as for a number of us who worked with or close to him; it was also a very significant chapter in the history of research into race and ethnicity.

In these brief comments, I want to reflect on just two aspects of the Cohen years – Robin's personal and administrative styles and his academic leadership. But, first, I would like to say a word about the general context of the Centre at Warwick.

The context

The research centre (which came to be known simply as CRER), developed out of the Race Research Unit based at Aston University in Birmingham, under the directorship of the late John Rex. This, however, was not merely a physical move from one university to another: the ESRC – the funders of the centre – and Warwick insisted on new leadership and a high level of academic production. In these circumstances, the new director, Robin, faced several challenges.

In that same year, 1984, I also joined Warwick as the Leverhulme Visiting Fellow in the newly established Centre for Caribbean Studies founded by the late Alistair Hennessy, Gad Heuman and Robin. In that year, I was on sabbatical from the University of the West Indies at Mona, Jamaica, and therefore had something of a front row seat to observe the settling-down of the two very different centres. However, as the year developed, it became clear that I was passing from being an observer of the quite exciting developments that were taking place and becoming a minor player. As a consequence of this, and encouraged by Robin, John Solomos, Malcolm Cross, John Rex and others, I did not return to the University of the West Indies but took up a post at CRER at the end of the fellowship. I stayed on at Warwick until 1994, when, long after Robin's departure from CRER it became clear to me that, as the Romans would say, my *dignitas* (as well as my health and sanity) demanded I beat a hasty retreat from Warwick and escape the new racial politics – largely from outside the centre – that had been engulfing CRER in the post-Cohen period.

While, therefore, the Cohen years 1984/5–1988/9 were characterized by an optimism to change the general context of how race issues were being researched, the post-Cohen years witnessed the control of the centre by ambitious men (and they were men!) from outside who saw the centre as a site from which to promote what appeared to be a benign racism from which their careers would prosper. By 1994, this had blown up in their faces and thereafter the end was almost inevitable. This is not the occasion to reflect on these disasters. Instead, let me say a word or two about Robin's personal and administrative styles.

Robin's administrative and personal styles

Robin inherited what must have been a difficult situation of leading an already largely formed group of researchers whose former leader remained a major player. My observation of Robin in these years was that he was determined not only to make a success of his new brief, but to do so without rancour. To this end, he displayed courtesy and charm; and he sought to ensure that all members of the centre were treated with due respect for their views about administrative matters as well as ownership of their work.

During his directorship (as before and after) Robin did not live in the two comfortable towns where Warwick academics ensconced themselves – Leamington and Kenilworth; neither did he join the few of us who had taken cover in and around Coventry. This gave him the capacity to spend an enormous amount of concentrated time outside working hours on the job. If you shared a task with Robin, you had to be on your toes or he would be finished long before you, and ready to compare and discuss notes. His presence also provided an opportunity to get to know Robin more closely, more informally, than you would do at the formal place of work. It was in this way that we learnt that we had more in common than having both lived and worked in Africa and the Caribbean: for a start both our wives are called Selina.

One of the major problems Robin inherited was that some individual researchers were failing to deliver on their specific research projects. To rectify this situation, Robin insisted on team leaders setting out – in collaboration with individuals – schedules that could be monitored, assessed and be seen to achieve targets. Part of this was to ensure that each researcher carried out the work they were employed to do, participate in the full life of the centre (for example in seminars and conferences) and develop a publication portfolio. In a work-culture where each individual felt that their production was their own affair, it was not an easy task to engender collaborative work with expected end products. Robin exuded a confidence in others that encouraged them to make this transition; his openness, approachability and non-antagonistic personality were qualities that enhanced his role as a supportive director.

Robin's academic leadership

These and other personal qualities were brought to the academic leadership Robin displayed in the directorship. I do not know, but I would guess that while he must have done much of the work for *The new helots* (1987) before coming to CRER, much of it must have been done while being director. I would also guess that at least some of the work for *Frontiers of identity* (1994) would have been done during those four years. In other words, the demands of administration did not stop the flow of work.

But there is a more important point to be borne in mind here: crucially, Robin did not attempt to make his intellectual concerns the sole driver of the work of the centre. This is important because Warwick as well as some of the advisers from outside the university became rather obsessed, particularly in the early 1990s, about some one person providing a central intellectual leadership for all researchers. This was a desire to return to an intellectually closed world in which one person's perspective strove to become the sole one – a not at all fruitful or healthy intellectual situation for social studies. Robin's approach was to veer more towards him being *primus inter pares*, and therefore more collegial than directorial.

Robin had come to the directorship from outside what was at the time derisively called 'the race relations industry', and this I believe enabled him to encourage the broadening of the *scope* of study. In the first place, the name was changed from 'race' to 'race and ethnic' relations, indicating a much needed clarity of the object of study as well as a correction of what kinds of relations were being studied. This reflected a shift from a predominant view that a person's or a group's 'racial' identity explained their consciousness and behaviour to the view that the values and beliefs, traditions and customs that make up our ethnic identities are paramount. This also marked a shift from the study of 'race' *per se* to 'racism'.

Now that such distinctions are well established and accepted, this shift may appear to be relatively trivial. But, in those decades, many progressive individuals in and outside academia – irrespective of what they may have professed – acted as if a person's singular racial identity determined their social being and behaviour.

The shift of focus from 'race' opened the way for a number of salutary developments. The new programme of research during Robin's four years (i) emphasized the need to study specific groups in Britain as they sought to establish themselves; (ii) identified specific problems, issues and initiatives along thematic lines so that they were researched in comparative terms; and, (iii) for perhaps the first time some researchers were encouraged to bring their research experiences outside Britain to bear on the British situation. This allowed for the *scope* of the field to be expanded and researchers came from a variety of disciplinary backgrounds. Individuals from political science, history, social geography and so forth came to the enterprise and, through the regular 'open seminars', publication series and visiting fellowships, interested parties from across the university, other universities in Britain and abroad, as well as local communities came to see CRER as a desirable destination and the proper site for discussing related issues. CRER had come to build up a critical mass of expertise to attract research students, offer a taught master's programme and, generally, take leadership of research and publication in the field both in Britain and in continental Europe.

One crucial aspect of Robin's leadership was that for perhaps the first time individual scholars and researchers from black and ethnic minority backgrounds felt comfortable working in such an environment. They were encouraged to apply for vacant posts and those appointed were appropriately promoted and given responsibilities. The overwhelming impression I had when I entered this area of research was that it had been a white preserve (like the rest of the university), intentionally or otherwise. During the Cohen years there began the shift to draw on talents irrespective of race and/or ethnicity. These developments were at one with the call for equality for all individuals following the Scarman Report into the Brixton disturbances in 1981. This was to change under the impact of protests over Salman Rushie's *Satanic Verses*; these protests marked a seismic shift in debates about race and ethnic matters in Britain: the new focus was to become the rights of religious communities. In these new circumstances, the university itself, as well as the funders of the centre, were only too ready to support the new expressions of rights and abandon the demand for each individual, each citizen, to be treated equally.

Conclusion

For me, one of the most noticeable things about Robin during those years was what I would call his *creative intellectual restlessness*. I believe that as soon as he saw that CRER was up and running, a going concern within the ESRC and Warwick world sites, he wanted to move on to pastures new and to break new ground. While his moving on led to major contributions on migration and diasporas, I have always felt that the window of opportunity that he opened as director of CRER was, unfortunately, closed soon after his departure. I have had the opportunity to call on him on several occasions for support thereafter, but by the mid-1990s much of the good work he had established had been institutionally undermined. Nonetheless, a good part of the high regard with which he is widely held properly arises from the work he quietly and efficiently conducted as director of CRER between 1984 and 1988.

6. Serial Offender: Robin Cohen as Editor of Journals and Books

Alisdair Rogers

I want to say something about an important but overlooked dimension of intellectual life, Robin's role as an editor and adviser on numerous book series and scholarly journals. I must begin by thanking Robin himself who, with typical wit and generosity, provided me with the title itself. My observations are in two parts. First, I shall provide something of an overview of Robin's labours in this field, speaking largely as a bystander or latecomer. Second, I would like to share some thoughts from our association – now 15 years or more – with the journal *Global Networks*.

Robin has been either an editor or on the advisory board of over a dozen book series, many of them of considerable significance. They're summarized in Table 1. I cannot claim to know them all well, but there are at least three I think should be singled out. The Sage Series on *African modernization and development* produced its first title in 1974 and, over the next six years, nine more were to follow. Robin (along with Gavin Williams) contributed to that first volume, *The political economy of contemporary Africa* edited by Peter Gutkind and Immanuel Wallerstein. Many authors and contributors to the series cultivated a distinct political economy take on African 'development', recasting it in terms of labour, slavery, peasantry, cities and trade. Looking back at those volumes, one is struck by the endurance of the insights they contained – or, at least, the continuing necessity of those insights.

Table 1: Books series associated with Robin Cohen

Book	Role	Dates
Sage Series on African Modernization and Development	Advisory Board	1978–84
Series on World Poverty, Toronto University Press	Advisory Board	1982–86
Zed Series on International Labour Studies	Series Editor	1982–87
Cambridge Series on Comparative Race & Ethnic Relations	Series Editor	1984–92
Cambridge Series on African Societies Today	Series Editor	1985–92
Cambridge Series on Third World Development	Advisory Board	1986–90
Series on Global Diasporas	Editor	1997–2011
Sage Handbook of Race and Ethnic Studies	Advisory Board	2004–6
Mondi Migranti: Soggetti, reti e movimento	Scientific Council	2006–
Migrations and Identities (Liverpool UP)	Editorial Board	2008–11
Theory for a Global Age (Bloomsbury)	Co-editor	2010–13
Migration, Diasporas and Citizenship (Palgrave)	Co-editor	2011–
Elgar International Library of Studies on Migration	Founding editor	1997–

A second collection I want to highlight is more recent, the UCL/Routledge series on global diaspora, starting of course with Robin's own vital contribution *Global diasporas: an introduction* (1997). I last counted a further eight titles, including Nick Van Hear's New *diasporas: the mass exodus, dispersal and regrouping of migrant communities* (1998). There is no need to explain to an audience here in Oxford, especially at the Martin School, how path breaking this series proved to be. It not only enabled various scholars to flesh out the revivified concept of diaspora with high quality research, but it also furthered the comparative dimension that was arguably absent from the classic cases.

We cannot overlook the weightiest contribution Robin has made as a book series editor, the now 19-volume Elgar Series of the *International Library of Studies on Migration*. I say 'weightiest' for good reason. Some of you may have seen that marvellous photograph of Robin holding the first 15 chunky tomes. I cannot tell whether he is smiling from merited satisfaction at the achievement, or grimacing at the strain on his back. We are told that they add up to more than 10,000 pages of material!

Robin's role as an editor, co-editor or advisory board member of journals is even more impressive. He has had some hand in at least 29 journals, 19 of which are still ongoing (Table 2). In a possibly misguided attempt to measure this activity, I estimated how many editor years Robin has accumulated. It is about 324. Moreover, if we make a simple assumption that each journal has four issues a year (and I know that the *Journal of Ethnic and Migration Studies* far exceed that) then this amounts to some 1296 complementary issues. By my reckoning, that is around ten metres of shelf space.

Table 2: Journals associated with Robin Cohen

Journal	Role	Dates
West African Journal of Politics and Sociology	Advisory Board	1974–78
Review of African Political Economy	Founding co-editor	1974–90
Working Papers on Caribbean Society	Founding editor	1978–80
Newsletter on International Labour Studies	Founding co-editor	1978–90
Cahiers d'études africaines	Advisory Board	1981–94
Labour, Capital & Society	Consultative Board	1982–
Development & Change	Advisory Board	1985–95
Migration: a European Journal of Migration & Ethnic Relations	Co-editor	1988–95
Journal of International Development	Advisory Board	1989–93
New Community/JEMS	Advisory Board	1989–2013
International Journal of Comparative Race & Ethnic Studies	Advisory Board	1994–
Caribbean Journal of Social Psychology & Criminology	Editorial Board	1995–
Social Identities	Editorial Board	1995–
International Review of Social History	Advisory Board	1995–2001
International Affairs	Advisory Board	1998–2010
Global Networks: a Journal of Transnational Affairs	Founding co-editor	2001–
Globalizations	Advisory Board	2004–?
Diaspora: a Journal of Transnational Studies	Advisory Board	2003–
Sikh Studies: an Interdisciplinary Journal	Advisory Board	2004–
Diasporas, histoire et societies	Advisory Board	2004–
Mobilities	Editorial Board	2005–14
Translocations	Advisory Board	2005–
University of Mauritius Research Journal	Advisory Board	2006–
Contemporary Politics	Editorial Board	2008–
Millennium: Journal of International Studies	Advisory Board	2008–
Crossings: Journal of Migration and Culture	Editorial Board	2010–
South African Review of Sociology	Advisory Board	2010–
Portuguese Journal of Political Science and International Relations	Advisory Board	2010–
Diaspora Studies	Advisory Board	2012

Three things strike me about this list of journals. First, there is the intellectual or disciplinary range: the titles embrace sociology, politics, culture, political economy, migration studies and many more fields. Second, there is a truly international scope. In addition to the roster of North American, Commonwealth and European, journals there are titles from Portugal and Mauritius. Third, although Robin's eminence has certainly led to his presence on a dozen or more advisory or international boards, he has also been active in the foundation of a number of titles. I will mention just one.

The *Review of African Political Economy* first appeared in 1974. The issue's contents page is reproduced in figure 1.

Figure 1: ROAPE first issue contents page

Number 1	Contents	
August-November 1974 (reprinted June 1978)	Editorial	1
Editorial Working Group Chris Allen Manfred Bienefeld Lionel Cliffe Ruth First Erica Flegg Mejid Hussein Duncan Innes Mustafa Khogali Peter Lawrence Katherine Levine Jitendra Mohan Gavin Williams	Accumulation and Development: A Theoretical Model Samir Amin	9
	Development or Exploitation: Is the Sahel Famine Good Business? Claude Meillassoux	27
	Feudalism, Capitalism and Famine in Ethiopia Lionel Cliffe	34
Overseas Editors Cairo: Shahida El Baz Copenhagen: Roger Leys Dar es Salaam: Mahmood Mamdani Trinidad: Robin Cohen Stockholm: Bhagavan, Bjorn Beckman Toronto: Jonathan Barker, John Saul Washington: Meredeth Turshen	African Peasants and Revolution John S. Saul	41
Contributing Editors Basil Davidson Sam Geza Thomas Hodgkin Charles Kallu-Kalumiya Colin Leys Robert van Lierop Archie Mafeje Claude Meillassoux Ken Post	Briefings Portugal and Africa: After the Lisbon Coup with extracts from Antonio Spinola, *Portugal and the Future* The Liberation of Mozambique and the Lisbon Coup Frelimo Notes on Race and Class Africa Information Services	69
Subscriptions (3 issues) UK Individuals £3.00 Institutions £4.50 Africa (except South Africa) Individuals £2.00/$4.00 Institutions £4.00/$8.00 Elsewhere Individuals £4.50/$9.00 Institutions £7.50/$15.00 Airmail extra £2.25/$4.50 Single copies Individuals £1.20/$3.50 Institutions £2.40/$7.00 Airmail-add £0.75/$1.50	Reviews	84
	Terminology: A Guide	89
	Radical Africana: A Bibliography Chris Allen	92
	Subscription to: Review of African Political Economy c/o Onyx Press 27 Clerkenwell Close London EC1R 0AT	

Figure 1 shows Robin as an Overseas Editor in Trinidad, though this is a reprint. In the original he is one of the 'Editorial Working Group' (a suitably collective title) along with Gavin Williams and Peter Lawrence, who I want to mention because he is also on the editorial board of *Global Networks*. And there are names there of colleagues now departed. I believe Robin and Peter edited the journal's special issue following the assassination of Ruth First in 1982. Like the Sage series I mentioned before, the journal brought to the fire the political economy of Africa, focusing on class inequality, liberation, the state, capital, exploitation and oppression – all still absolutely apposite in my opinion. It is still going more than forty years later (though will cost you £52 to subscribe, not the original £3).

I speak now as the chief editor of a journal. I believe that journal editing, including the part played by advisory editors, is a necessary labour in academia. That remains the case even with the spread of open access publishing. Nevertheless, it is not fêted and for the most part, not tangibly rewarded. Why then has Robin contributed so spectacularly? And why does he continue to do so? I note that a dozen or more of the titles with which he is associated were begun since 2000, by which time it might well be thought that he had earned some reprieve. This can only be speculation, but I can only think that it involves at least three kinds of motivation. There must be an undiminished enthusiasm for sharing scholarship, for spreading ideas and generating responses. This is, after all, the very stuff of academic life. Second, Robin has shown a commitment to various overlapping communities, helping to sustain them and bring them into contact with one another. If I had the time, and the necessary computational skill, I would chart the network of 'interlocking boards' created through Robin's editorial interventions. Third, performing the editorial role is an example of service to scholarship. It is an act of citizenship (which I think gets bastardized as 'esteem' in our RAE/REF times). I am aware that the term 'service' conjures up associated ideas of duty and sacrifice, terms about which we should be cautious. However, I do not think they are out of place in this context.

I now turn to *Global Networks*, enabling me to escape from lists and numbers and speak from more personal experience. The link between us was forged by Steve Vertovec. Steve and Robin were together at the Centre for Research in Ethnic Relations (CRER) at the University of Warwick. I was friends with Steve from Nuffield College, where we were both supervised by the anthropologist Clyde Mitchell. My first sense of Robin in anything other than the sense of a sociologist whose work I really ought to read came from some praise Steve passed on from Robin to the effect that the introduction I had written to *The urban context* (Berg 1995) was 'great'. I was quietly chuffed. Robin of course helped Steve put together the case for what was to become the ESRC Programme on Transnational Communities, which brought Steve back to Oxford as its director in 1997. Being a stipendiary lecturer in human geography at various Oxford colleges at the time, I was grateful for the chance to be asked to work behind the scene on a research programme as a 'consultant.'

In the programme's offices on the top floor of a building on Bevington Road, Robin and Steve continued what I can only describe as a very 'generative' relationship: I mean they had – and still have – a lot of great ideas. Among them, in around 1999, was the idea of starting a new journal to showcase some of the research coming out of the programme's 18 independent projects. *Global Networks* took shape around three main strands then current in the common ground between anthropology, sociology and geography (our three particular disciplines). These were globalization in its broadest and, then, sexiest formulations; transnationalism, coming out of migration studies but also leaching into other kinds of communities, for example, criminal, professional and protest; networks, especially inspired by Manuel Castells's flawed but generative three-volumes on the network society. The journal did not turn out quite as we imagined it (we envisaged something more like *International Affairs*) but, even so, it has done pretty well if I may say so.

What were the qualities that Robin brought to *Global Networks*? He had a clear intellectual vision for the journal, not just in the sense of a coherent programme of research questions but also in the sense of an 'elevator pitch'. The journal had to be sold to publishers, first Routledge and then Blackwell. I recall Robin encapsulating the journal's aims in terms of the contrast between twentieth-century internationalism and twenty-first century transnationalism. It proved persuasive, and it also helped me focus on what we were trying to do. When it came to assembling the editorial board and team of regional and associate editors, it was of considerable help that Robin was able to draw upon an amazing global network of friends, colleagues and contacts – among them Patricia Mohammed, Paul Kennedy and Jimi Adesina with us today. Closer to home, I believe a conversation across a garden wall in North Oxford landed us our first meeting with Routledge. In addition to Robin's enthusiasm and vigour for the journal, there is another quality I wish to single out. If you have been lucky enough to visit Robin and Selina in their Oxford home, you will appreciate that they have a good eye for painting. Blackwell had come up with some ideas for the journal cover, but they were fairly predictable and frankly dull: globes with arching and whizzing trajectories. In a meeting with the publishers, it was Robin who drew the three overlapping globes on a piece of paper that eventually became the cover. I think it is a great cover, simple and striking.

Figure 2: *Global Networks* covers

That was in 1999. Some 56 issues later Robin remains a wise counsellor, reviewer, finder of referees, negotiator with publishers and proofreader of *Global Networks*. His commitment gives me very considerable reassurance. And when you get Robin's support, you also get Selina and Jason. As Oxford Publishing Services, Selina has been utterly rigorous in policing the articles' grammar, punctuation and spelling while Jason has crafted the manuscripts into perfect camera-ready copy and dealt with the odd recalcitrant author. I hope you will indulge a human geographer and forgive my pretension if I call to mind a sociologist whose influence extends to my own discipline – Pierre Guillaume Frédéric Le Play. He's known for his dictum place–work–family. Oxford is the place, editing is the work and I feel fortunate to be part of Robin's 'family' of colleagues.

7. Montreal and the Journal, *Labour, Capital and Society/Travail, capital et société*

Rosalind Boyd

What a wonderful occasion this is to celebrate 'all things Robin', a creative mind with a great sense of humour, a generous spirit always encouraging one's ideas and pursuits, as a well-grounded critical scholar *par excellence*. That is how I recall Robin and view his influence from my base at McGill's Centre for Developing-Area Studies (CDAS) in Montreal, particularly in the 1970s and 1980s when he was a frequent guest. As we shall hear in tomorrow's presentations, Robin helped to shift the study of international labour from too narrow or too abstract or ahistorical interpretations to a needed examination of the complexity of the actual conditions that the labouring people in societies of the so-called 'Third World' were experiencing. With us in Montreal, he set out new approaches to the study of labour through questioning the prevailing notions or orthodoxy, always digging deeper. By so doing, he helped us to found the CDAS/McGill-based academic bilingual journal, *Labour, Capital and Society/Travail, capital et société: A journal on the Third World* in 1979. Some of the terrain and his approach are reflected in *Peasants and proletarians: the struggles of third world workers* (1979) co-edited with the late Peter Gutkind and Phyllis Brazier and our jointly co-edited book also done with Peter Gutkind, *International labour and the third world: the making of a new working class* published in 1987, the same year Robin published *The new helots*.

In that latter book, he acknowledged Peter Gutkind and me as among 'friends that had reawakened an interest in inter-national labour issues'. We always attributed Robin's frequent presence in Montreal as developing or reinforcing our focus on international labour issues. But, as you well know, that is the nature of genuine intellectual exchange where you do not always recognize where the ideas, the insights, the creative responses spring from or who is to be attributed, especially when the exchanges are respectful, informed and often very passionate, as they were with Robin. In addition, published scholarly works, while important, give only a fraction of what constitutes the social activity around the research; what is hidden or left out often rises to the surface on occasions like this. Robin was able to bring to our attention what we were embarking on even before we were sure of it. He did this by asking many insightful questions and looking critically at the real world, sensing the complexity of what is really going on or has gone on. He seemed to move between a critique of the published texts and notions of Marx and a host of others (including Saul and Arrighi), while observing the world in all its intricacies.

Ros Boyd with Robin and Selina Cohen,
Warwick, 1989 ROAPE Conference

I have not actually been in Robin's company since 1989 at the ROAPE conference 'Taking Democracy Seriously in Africa' held at Warwick where I presented my early research on Uganda, when the National Resistance Movement under Museveni was establishing an enabling environment for women. Mahmood Mamdani and his Labour Studies Group at Makerere had invited me to Uganda in 1987 and I had gone again in 1988. I recall how Robin encouraged my research and, unknown to me, organized ROAPE to publish that first version of my article 'Empowerment of Women in Contemporary Uganda: Real or Symbolic?' Over the years, I have followed his nomadic journey physically and intellectually to the Caribbean, back to South Africa and finally to England again. His research is always grounded in a passionate concern for a deeper understanding of the marginalized, the uprooted, the migrants, and the helots of the world who today need to be understood with greater urgency and attention, especially with the overt predominance of racial profiling we are witnessing or experiencing.

In my presentation I shall situate Robin's interaction with us in Montreal in that early period, for tomorrow we shall focus more on the debates related to labour studies. First, I shall provide some background to the founding of *Labour, Capital and Society* (*LCS*) in the 1970s with three key moments (1968, 1975 and then 1979/80); then a little about the Montreal context and finally where *LCS/TCS* is now. I shall briefly touch on Robin's impact on me personally.

Background to founding LCS

It is important first to recall the early research activities at CDAS, particularly those guided by the late Peter Gutkind, a noted anthropologist who, primarily in Africa, had conducted research on urbanization and the urban poor. Robin's involvement was key to the debates we were having in the 1970s and much of this history has been lost with the closure of CDAS. In 1968, Peter G., as we affectionately referred to him, had started a newsletter on unemployment research in Africa with two other anthropologists, André Lux (Laval University) and Peter Carstens (University of Toronto). I had reluctantly taken on this newsletter in 1972 or 1973 and was slowly transforming it into a more scholarly journal. Then, in May 1975, Peter organized an international workshop in Montreal at McGill and invited Robin to participate along with other noted left leaning progressive scholars (Ken Post, Peter Waterman, Colin Leys, Francisco Zapata, Hamza Alavi and Myron Echenberg among others). I believe that was the first time Robin came to Montreal. Their presentations, which established our CDAS Working Paper Series, defined one of the dominant research clusters – critical development studies with the labouring people as its focus – that was emerging at our graduate research centre. Robin's presentation was entitled 'Marxism and Africa: Old, New and Projected' (which was rather similar to his 1972 *Socialist Register* article). From 1975 until the departure of Peter G. from CDAS and McGill in 1986 to Warwick, Robin was a frequent guest lecturer and visitor to Montreal.[1] Those years also established the great friendship between Robin and Peter G. as well as us in Montreal.

During that 1970s period, we had also formed a non-hierarchical multidisciplinary Labour Studies Group (LSG) of graduate students, researchers and faculty based at the CDAS. We received funding from the Quebec government to host a yearlong series of seminars during the academic year 1979/80 ending with a major conference on International Labour Issues in May 1980. When planning these events, Robin attended some of our LSG meetings in Montreal; he was generous in helping to identify new scholars and critical themes in preparation for both the seminars and the international conference. Then, in 1979, he gave the opening keynote lecture, 'The "New" International Labour Studies: A Definition' at CDAS, which set the stage for dozens of subsequent seminars and debates that continue up until today.[2]

---

1. Robin gave another important lecture related to critical sociology entitled 'Sociology and development literature: a critical overview' published in 1985 as CDAS Discussion Paper no. 26.
2. This was reprinted three times in the CDAS Working Paper Series, no. 27, 1980. It was then modified for publication in our 1987 book, *International labour* and Robin's 1991 book, *Contested domains*.

Activism and solidarity with various liberation struggles of the so-called Third World, and now labelled the global South, were integral to what we were doing in Montreal and were embedded in our scholarship. Our approach was not always favoured by those at the CDAS or McGill and disapproval was often reflected in a strange manner. For example, when we organized the opening reception at McGill's Faculty Club for that international conference in May 1980, staff members there wondered what kind of motley group had invaded or taken over; they were still accustomed to suits and ties, with mainly men. Many women were participants in this conference (such as Jane Parpart, Georgina Jaffe, Paula Bailey, Sharon Stichter, Nirmala Banerjee and others). Women were still not regular members of the Faculty Club though the first woman was admitted in 1936.

We combined our research activities with those of the other universities in Quebec and the wider international community, placing those from the regions of the global South at the centre. We joined the 1 May demonstration in the streets of Montreal with workers' organizations and other social movements during that conference. We included important labour acti-vists from the South in that conference, notably Guillermo Lora from Bolivia as well as Irfan Habib, a Marxist labour historian from India and Pablo Gonzalez Casanova, a well-known Mexican sociologist and noted labour historian of Latin America, among others. I believe that Robin was the one to draw our attention to the *South African Labour Bulletin* and the work of Eddie Webster who also attended the 1980 conference and subsequently published his first article in *LCS/TCS* in 1981,[3] which had been banned in South Africa. Later, in my

---

3. '"Stay-aways" and the black working class: evaluating a strategy'.

last issue as editor in 2004, 'Celebrating 25 years of *LCS/TCS*', Eddie wrote in his article that that interaction with *LCS* was vital in bringing labour struggles in apartheid South Africa to an international audience and that this 1980 conference event was the beginning of a lifelong network of contacts.[4] Over the years, *LCS* published dozens of articles and some special issues related to South Africa.[5]

In 1972, as mentioned, I had somewhat reluctantly taken over the editorship of the Newsletter *Manpower (sic) and Unemployment Research in Africa.* What kind of feminist works on a Newsletter with the word 'manpower' in its title! Despite the title, we were publishing some very fine articles. These included Samir Amin's 'Underpopulated Africa', Terrance McGee's 'Hawkers and Hookers in Southeast Asia, Isidore M'Baye Dieng's study of a squatter settlement in Dakar, Bernard Bernier's sub-proletariat in Quebec to cite but a few. Robin's article entitled 'The Politics of Unemployment in Mauritius' was published in 1978 under the old name.

We, along with others based in Montreal, Quebec City and Toronto, debated the broadening of the title beyond 'unemployment' to reflect this wider terrain, what we were actually publishing. In 1979, with Robin's influence and support from

---

4. See his article in the 37 (1–2) 2004 issue of *LCS*. These Montreal events were also Ronnie Munck's first acquaintance with our research and led him to work in Durban some years later and become a regular contributor to *LCS/TCS*. Ronnie, who is here today, participated in the 1979 seminar series and later published *The new international labour studies: an introduction* (London: Zed Books, 1988) for which Robin wrote the Foreword.

5. As editor, I recognized that two major struggles of that period – the liberation of Palestine and the liberation of apartheid South Africa – were vital to address.

others,[6] we turned *Labour, Capital and Society: A Journal on the Third World* into a respected academic journal to reflect the wider regional coverage and the many thematic interpretations of international labour. Peter G. continued to provide a bibliographical section on unemployment until about 1990.

Robin always reinforced rigorous scholarship and helped many of us establish a link between well-founded research and activism. He also taught us to recognize the multifaceted conditions of labouring people in the less-developed regions. This pursuit was helped by members of the wider progressive intellectual community at the other three Montreal universities who found refuge at the CDAS, where Peter G. was 'our front man' for a wide range of alternative scholarly cum activism activities.

We also, from 1979 to 1988/9, published a *Register of Ongoing Labour Research*, which identified a large network of researchers worldwide, a global network of contributors to the journal particularly in those regions. It is necessary to recall that we were working prior to the internet and e-mail connections and built our network through direct personal contacts.[7]

Montreal context

In those early years, we also tapped into the many researchers and networks identified by Peter Waterman,[8] but our Montreal

---

6. Including Immanuel Wallerstein, Jose Nun, Jean Copans and Peter Waterman, among others.
7. A remarkable number of labour studies groups were being established worldwide, often in universities such as Mamdani's group at Makerere, which later became the independent Centre for Basic Research in Kampala. When I was based at CODESRIA in 1983, I was surprised to come across some dusty copies of *LCS/TCS* in a library in St Louis, the old capital of Senegal outside Dakar.
8. See the bibliography section in our 1987 book *International labour*.

context was different. I am unsure how much impact we or Montreal, which is a cosmopolitan multilingual city with a large number of immigrants, refugees, asylum seekers and exiles (especially from Chile, Argentina, Vietnam and Haiti) had on Robin. *LCS/TCS* was based at a graduate research centre on development or developing areas with a significant number of graduate students from Africa, Asia, the Caribbean and Latin America and professors who had worked in these regions.[9] Despite the constant difficulties we experienced at the CDAS and McGill, we affirmed that our international labour orientation was part of scholarship within development, part of dislodging the mainstream canons of the time, especially modernization and the various detached economic paradigms dominant at most universities. Transformational scholarship was bound to be subversive. As well, we were working outside disciplinary boundaries, outside those silos, which is possible at a research centre.

We were located in the French-speaking Province of Quebec where the separatist Parti Québécois had had its first victory in 1976 under René Lévesque. The first referendum on separation – or more precisely sovereignty association – took place in 1980; we were in the midst of radical changes in Quebec where vibrant protests were reflected in the streets and in the popular culture. Yet, we were based at conservative McGill, the oldest English university in Canada with few making any outreach to the Francophone intellectual community that was part of our core group. In fact, *LCS* was published from the French Université

---

9. The Caribbean region was especially significant in those years when C. L. R. James and others were visitors to Montreal, documented in a recently published book by David Austin, *Fear of a black nation* (Toronto: Between the Lines Press, 2013).

de Montreal for three years (1989–91) when I tried to resign the first time. Robin may not have agreed with all that we did at CDAS and published in *LCS/TCS*, but he was a major catalyst to the underlying process of what we were doing. In rereading his early critical work on international labour, I would say that our published work and research activities fit somewhere into the spectrum of the progressive left tradition and we were often 'overtly engaged and committed' but not usually 'orthodox'.

From time to time, we reflected on the direction of labour studies and what we were publishing in *LCS*. For example, in April 1988, we published two such contributions – Peter Wad focused on labour studies in East and Southeast Asia and Francisco Zapata surveyed labour studies in Latin America. In a previous issue (November 1987), Bill Freund contributed a review article 'Recent Work on Labour in Africa'. These appraisals of labour studies built on, or were impacted by, that classic 1979 lecture 'The New International Labour Studies: A Definition', which had been widely circulated and which emphasized the importance of seeing diversity in the labour struggles of these regions, 'digging deeper' when conducting the research.

Some reflections on my 25 years as editor and photos from that 1980 international conference event in Montreal in which Robin played a starring role are contained in my final issue published in 2004. Robin's article 'Chinese cockle-pickers, the transnational turn and everyday cosmopolitanism: reflections on the new global migrants' is published in that 2004 issue; the article is a prelude to his 2006 book *Migration and its enemies: global capital, migrant labour and the nation-state*. Some of the back issues are on the current *LCS* website and soon *JSTOR* will have all the articles available digitally. Most noted in the 1990s are the various special guest edited issues on child labour, on petty commodity production, South African miners, health and safety in the labour process, women and work in South Asia. There were also some remarkable early articles on worker consciousness (by Jimi Adesini 1989 who is here today), labour history, labour migration patterns, women in the labour process, unpaid labour, forms of labour resistance, the informal sector, proletarianization and sub-proletariats, trade unions, and so on.

Even from afar, Robin was always to be counted on to support our international labour studies activities – questioning, affirming and offering critical input – especially in the first ten years of establishing the journal when few development journals were addressing the struggles of the labouring people from the alternative perspective we advocated.

LCS/TCS now

In 2005, the journal moved from McGill to St Mary's University in Halifax and has continued under the able editorship of Suzanne Dansereau, who is an associate professor of international development there and a long-time labour researcher noted especially for her research on Zimbabwe and mining communities. Robin and Suzanne are well acquainted because she was a graduate student at McGill and at the Université du Québec à Montréal (UQAM) as well as one of the coordinators of the Labour Studies Group in the early years, and has been a member of the *LCS* editorial committee since 1996. Suzanne also guest edited a special issue, 'Zimbabwe: Independence and Beyond', dedicated to our beloved friend Peter G. who died on 17 February 2001. Robin remains an important consultative board member, along with many others from those early years.

After more than three decades of neoliberal globalization, which has brought greater inequalities and disrupted livelihoods of scores of people in all regions of the world, the new editor is gradually taking the journal in another direction to address international labour issues in the current context. However, the articles are still heavily influenced by the thematic debates and approach that Robin opened up so many years ago.

Whether directly cited or not, Robin's influence or impact can still be felt. For example, volume 41 (2) in 2008 has a special focus on resistance. The editor writes that 'in this period of increased intolerance, in which dissent and resistance are increasingly linked to terrorism, there is a need to conceptualize the nature of current resistance more broadly and the role of the labour movement within it. A broader conceptualization of resistance is required.' The global context is different but the theme is not. A 2006 special issue by Dolores Chew on 'Gender, Migration and Trafficking' examines a theme that was similar to her special issue ten years earlier, but the circumstances, she states, had worsened considerably. Similarly, under the new editor, *LCS/TCS* continues to publish research that critically questions labour in independent South Africa, building on the previously published articles. *LCS* has always relied on a small core of people dedicated to challenging the inequities in our world. Significantly, an article published in a recent special issue 'New Voices on Labour: Precarity and Resistance'[10] received the 2013 award for best-published article from the Working Class Studies Association, an association established in 2005. Tomorrow I hope to participate in the debates about labour

---

10. *LCS/TCS* 45, no. 1, 2012 guest edited by Aziz Choudry and Thomas Collombat.

studies and where the discipline might be going, especially whether 'globalization' has taken us to a significantly different place.

Robin's personal impact

Now permit me to be a little more personal about Robin before I end. After Robin's first visit to Montreal in 1975, I recall on one of his later visits a group of us going to a dinner party at the home of my dearest friends, Vera, a sculptor, and Paolo Vivante, a well-known Homeric scholar and professor of classics at McGill, where the wine flowed and conversations carried on deep into the night. Robin told stories about St Helena and, to this day, when I ask friends 'what do you remember about Robin?' they remember him as a great storyteller. For many years after, Paolo would ask, 'what happened to that fellow Robin Cohen? He told us such remarkable stories about St Helena.'[11] At the Gutkind's home and that of Margie Mendell,[12] there were occasions for good conversations not just about the state of the world or about Nigeria, where we had both worked and lived – me in Abeokuta, the birthplace of Wole Soyinka, and Robin in Ibadan – but also about Mauritius and Trinidad, both places dear to me.

Ironically, many of us also affectionately joked that he would be the first '*Sir* Robin Cohen' in our network, as Robin seemed,

---

11. We laughed about how my maternal ancestor, Henry Porteous, had put up Napoleon at his residence on his first night in St Helena.
12. She was a LSG member as a McGill Ph.D. economics student, on the editorial board of LCS, later co-founder of the Karl Polanyi Institute in Montreal and recently awarded the Prix de Ordre du Quebec (2013) related to her work on the social economy of Quebec and her work through the School of Community and Public Affairs at Concordia University.

to those of us based outside England or in Francophone North America to be rather anglicized. Now I think it might have been more about his ancestral Cohen heritage that was reasserting its 'priestly' class character. Who knows?[13] Robin's influence was felt in many ways apart from *Labour, Capital and Society*.[14] For example, reading *Contested domains* in 1992 helped me to find a clearer focus for my doctoral thesis, which dealt with emergent intellectual challenges to Western cultural hegemony in post-colonial societies. Whether intended or not, his work reaffirmed my confidence or validation of 'experiential knowledge' and also of negating certain texts – what Edward Said refers to as the 'misapprehension of the sources of authority'– if one is going to write from the perspective of the liberating process.

Robin had written about the complexity in the 'interplay between control and resistance ... in the real world' (page 15), which I perhaps took in an unintended direction. Other examples of his influence are more difficult to document as reading his texts and recalling the conversations we had with Peter G., with members of the Labour Studies Group and editorial committee of *LCS*[15] often live in an unconscious way just below the surface as material for understanding or questioning the human condition. The Canadian literary critic

---

13. I am most likely influenced by reading Samir Amin's autobiography which begins 'Ancestors do matter' or maybe the Montreal-born songwriter, singer and poet Leonard Cohen. [At this point the author gave Robin a present of Leonard Cohen's recent CD.]
14. Or all the debates about labour and Africa, which will be discussed tomorrow.
15. Margie Mendell, Myron Echenberg, Victor Piche, Pierre Beaucage, Rodolphe De Koninck, Myron Frankman, Joseph Mugore, Dolores Chew, Ayse Trak, Paresh Chattopadyay, Jonathan Barker, Gavin Smith and a host of others.

Northrop Frye said somewhere (maybe in *The educated imagination*) that influences are 'vagrant seeds blown towards a responsive soil'; that seems to fit Robin's influence on many of us at our base in Montreal. Maybe we too had some impact on him. What I vividly recall is that whenever Robin visited, many of us there in Montreal would be left inspired. Such is the nature of his superb character and intellectual energy.

Thank you for inviting me to this event and thank you Robin for all the remarkable and good things you are.

THEMES AND THREADS

8. The Interaction between Race and Colonialism: A Case Study of the Liverpool Race Riots of 1919

Roy May and Robin Cohen

Discussions of race relations in this country have primarily focused on the post-1945 situation when large-scale immigration from the black countries of the Commonwealth began. While scholarly concern for the postwar period is generally well-founded, this has usually meant that the origins, character and early manifestations of race conflict have had little systematic analysis. Considerable insights on these issues can be gleaned from the early works of Michael Banton, Kenneth Little and Anthony Richmond,[1] while more recently James Walvin has provided a narrative history of black–white relations in this country from 1555 to 1945.[2]

From these secondary sources alone, it is abundantly clear that the conventional wisdom that amicable relations existed prior to the postwar wave of immigration is unfounded. In our discussion of the Liverpool events of 1919 we have, through

---

1. Michael Banton, *The coloured quarter* (London, 1955); Kenneth K. Little, *Negroes in Britain* (London, 1948: new edition 1972); Anthony H. Richmond, *Colour prejudice in Britain* (London, 1954) and Anthony H. Richmond, *The colour problem* (Harmondsworth, 1955).
2. James Walvin, *Black and white: the Negro and English society 1555–1945* (London, 1973).

using primary source material, been able to provide richer and more complete data regarding one manifestation of racial conflict. But, more explicitly than the writers just cited, we have been conscious of the wider inferences that can be drawn from this series of events, and the value studies of this kind may have in providing support for an emerging set of concepts defining the sociology of race relations in the United Kingdom. To be more concrete:

1. The Liverpool events vividly demonstrate the intimate link between the origins of racism in Britain and the worldwide involvement of the metropolitan country in her colonial Empire.
2. What happened in Liverpool should be seen in relation to the contemporaneous emergence of a transnational black consciousness. Though the actors in our Liverpool scenario were, more often than not, oblivious of such connections, some observers perceived that the central fact of white superordination and black subordination lent the expressions of racial dissent in many parts of the world a common significance, if not a common cause.

The effect of the colonial experience on the growth of racism had a dual impact. On the one hand, racial theories that by the turn of the century had assumed a material force in their own right were used to legitimize relationships of dominance and disability within the Empire.[3] On the other hand, the very

---

3. In the context of Nigeria, for example, James Coleman writes that 'color discrimination was the product not only of preconceptions regarding African inferiority, reinforced by a magnification of the faults of educated Africans, but also of the firm conviction that

achievement of military superiority and administrative control over the colonized peoples fed back to the metropolis in the form of stereotypes, mythologies and ideologies that confirmed the supposed superiority of the Anglo-Saxon 'race'.[4]

This causal interconnection between Empire and metropolis in the development of racial attitudes and practice leads us to concur with John Rex in arguing that race issues cannot merely be conceptualized in terms of an 'urban crisis' or propositions concerning the difficulties 'strangers' have in meeting the demands and expectations of a 'host' community.[5] While Rex and several scholars are conscious of the salience of the colonial experience in explaining the origins of racism in the UK, our discussion of the Liverpool riots provides some historical specificity, which, generally speaking, has been left unexplored. It is notable, too, how several areas of contemporary debate – the attitudes of the trade unions, the role of the police, the question of repatriation – were raised initially during the events of 1919.

The race riots in Liverpool in June 1919 were paralleled by similar events in Cardiff, Barry, Newport, London and Manchester. The period immediately following the First World

---

peaceful colonial administration and the perpetuation of imperial rule were directly dependent upon the doctrine of white superiority.' James S. Coleman, *Nigeria: background to nationalism* (Berkeley and Los Angeles, 1963), p. 152.

4. One pervasive example in the sphere of popular fiction is the work of G. A. Henty, who wrote over one hundred novels for boys. He extolled British military prowess and thought that 'the intelligence of the average negro is about equal to that of a European child of ten years old.' See G. D. Killam, *Africa in English fiction, 1874–1939* (Ibadan, 1968) Chapter II.

5. J. Rex, *Race, colonialism and the city* (London, 1973).

War was one of great social disturbance in several parts of the world. In Liverpool itself, traditional constraints broke down not only in respect of race relations but also in respect of those who might be expected to be the most stalwart defenders of the social order. During August bank holiday, the police themselves went on strike and their protest was only quashed after tanks and three battalions were moved into the city and a battleship and destroyers sailed up the River Mersey.[6] This kind of overreaction by the British government is explicable in terms of a general fear of the social dislocation of the bloody and protracted war and the ideological alternative posed by the success of the Bolsheviks in Russia. Though the threat turned out to be exaggerated, it did produce a feeling that social dissent happening in one part of the world had a direct effect in another. In the colonies, administrators were wont to attribute dissatisfaction to the work of outsiders – the demonology usually being either the communists or the Pan-Africanists, while at home many observers pointed out that racial disturbances in England would have serious repercussions for the European presence in the colonized world.

In section II we describe the Liverpool disturbances of 1919, try to identify the major causes of the riots and analyse the reactions of the police, national authorities and commentators to these events. In section III we describe, albeit briefly, manifestations of racial antagonism in other parts of the world, and show how some supporters of the Empire were conscious that racial violence was a phenomenon that, if left unchecked, could badly damage the legitimacy of the colonial

---

6. G. W. Reynolds and A. Judge, *The night the police went on strike* (London, 1968).

administration in the eyes of its subjects. A short conclusion follows in section IV.

II

The race riots in Liverpool took place in three main phases – an initial foray in May, the main events in June (which are described in detail), and a few subsequent incidents. In May, disturbances broke out after the Liverpool police had fought a running battle, with blacks involved in operating an illegal gaming house. Later incidents also were, on the surface, connected with criminal activity. In early June, for example, three white men were sentenced at Manchester Assizes for the robbery of £100 from an Indian?[7] Again in July, the Under Secretary of State for the Colonies was asked at Question Time in the Commons whether he was aware of the assault and robbery in Liverpool of three Gold Coast citizens who had arrived from Accra the day before.

Such incidents were symptomatic of a deeper breakdown in relations between the indigenous white population and Commonwealth citizens and aliens, whose presence in the major ports was considerably added to by a large number of discharged sailors. The major events in June began with a fracas between a number of blacks and white aliens. It seems that a black had been stabbed by a Scandinavian sailor on 4 June. Some blacks retaliated, first by throwing beer over some Scandinavians in a Liverpool bar, then, as they left the premises, the Scandinavians, 'were assailed by the coloured men with sticks, knives, razors

---

7. Walvin, op. cit., p. 206; *Liverpool Daily Post and Mercury* (2 June 1919).

and pieces of iron taken from lampposts; eight Scandinavians were taken to hospital and the coloureds headed for the Scandinavians' home in Great George Square',[8] white attacks on the black population followed. Police were called in to deal with these disturbances and in the ensuing fights four policemen were injured, two by revolver shots. Raids took place at a number of boarding houses. As Police Inspector Burgess laconically announced, 'in a number of houses [police] found coloured men apparently sleeping whom they took into custody'.[9] In one of these boarding houses was a Bermudan, Charles Wotten, who had served as a fireman in the Royal Navy. He fled from the police and was drowned in the Queen's Dock to cries of 'Let him drown!' from the mob.

Further trouble occurred in the next few days. Several blacks were charged with disorderly behaviour and assault on the police. One of the prisoners was seen to run along the street shouting 'down with the white race', while another, with the unlikely name of Sunny John, was accused of slashing a policeman with a razor. According to a report in *The Times*: 'white men appear[ed] determined to clear out the blacks who have been advised to stay indoors. This counsel many of them disregarded. ... Whenever a negro was seen he was chased and if caught severely beaten.'[10] Victims of white violence argued that as they were being 'discharged from their jobs and turned out from their lodgings, they could hardly avoid being seen on the street'.

Another incident, in Russell Street, concerned 'a coloured gentleman of good position' from one of the Liverpool liners

---

8. *Daily Post* (11 June 1919); *Liverpool Weekly Post* (21 June 1919).
9. *Liverpool Post* (6 June 1919), Richmond, op. cit., 1955, p. 285.
10. *The Times* (10 June 1919).

who had his car stopped and £175 taken. Apart from such attacks on (individuals, a lodging house on Jack Street was wrecked by a crowd of 2000. More riots were reported in Stanhope and Hill Street and there were attacks on the Elder Dempster Shipping Company Boarding House. Many blacks sought shelter with the police and, by 10 June, the police held 700 blacks for their own safety, with more arriving hourly. The Ethiopian Hall, run by the Liverpool Ethiopian Association, sheltered a further 70. Attacks by the white community became increasingly indiscriminate, as a letter to the *Liverpool Echo* by a Philipino illustrates. He pleaded that people should not 'vent their spite on any darker skin', and pointed out that 30 Philipinos were permanently settled in Liverpool, while seven of their number had been killed fighting for Britain during the war.[11]

With the active intervention of the police in separating the two sides, the most violent expressions of antagonism abated.

In August 1919, events took a slightly more bizarre turn with a 'deliberate and concerted attack' on a firm of export bottlers, J. P. O'Brien and Sons, a company with West African connections and some African employees. Though the identity of the intruders is not made clear by contemporary sources, the implication is that many blacks were involved. The journal *West Africa* reported the incident as follows. The raiders,

> to a number of a few scores, which soon grew into hundreds, forced their way into the establishment and helped themselves liberally to the various classes of liquor available. By the time the feast had led to the partial

---

11. *Liverpool Echo* (11 June 1919).

prostration of some of the participants, handcarts had
arrived, and what could not be consumed was carted
away.

The liquor was taken to the looters' headquarters, 'where consumption proceeded to the utmost capacity. After that the
enterprising offspring of the looters essayed into the streets and
sold bottles of beer at a penny apiece.'[12]

The interplay between more deep-rooted and immediate
causes of the riots are complex, but four main explanations were
either proffered at the time or are central to our understanding
of the riots. First, a feeling of sexual competition and the fear of
miscegenation on the part of the white population; second, the
concentrated and exposed nature of black settlement in
Liverpool – blacks being a readily identifiable minority; third,
an explanation that saw the outbreak of the disturbances simply
in terms of the exploitation by hooligan elements of the
unsettled conditions of the time; and finally, competition for
employment between the black and white communities. While
we discuss each explanation below, we are concerned also to
show an underlying link between the experience of Empire and
the manifestation of racial antipathy in the metropolis.

Walvin argues that the issue of sexual jealousy was evident
as early as the eighteenth and nineteenth centuries,[13] the
relationship of black men with white girls in particular arousing
hostile feelings. *The Times* commented on this issue as follows.

In the postwar situation many [blacks] married Liverpool

---

12. *West Africa* (16 August 1919) p. 705.
13. Walvin, op. cit., p. 208.

women and while it is admitted that some of them made good husbands the intermarriage of black men and white women, not to mention other relationships, has excited much feeling.[14]

The tone of moral condemnation was perhaps best expressed in the Cardiff riots, when the mob entering a house thought to be occupied by blacks were confronted by four white girls in night attire, saying 'we are British girls.' The intruders' reply was, 'thank God there are others.'[15]

The widespread influence of Social Darwinism, which had underpinned discriminatory colonial policies, was illustrated in an exchange of views in *The Times*. Claiming to speak for the vast majority of British men and women with experience overseas, Sir Ralph Williams, a former administrator in the West Indies and Bechuanaland, argued that to anyone who had spent some time in the colonies, intimate association between black and white was a thing of horror:

Every one of us has, probably, many friends among the coloured people, whom we bear in our kindliest remembrance. ... It does not, either, I think, arise from any feeling of social superiority. The cause is far deeper. It is an instinctive certainty that sexual relations between white women and coloured men revolts our very nature.

Sir Ralph thought it inevitable in the absence of their wives that black men's passions 'should run high after a period of long

---

14. *The Times* (10 June 1919).
15. *The Times* (13 June 1919).

abstinence'. [16] No doubt he thought white district officers were made of sterner stuff.

The General Secretary of the Society of Peoples of African Origin (London), F. E. M. Hercules, wrote a rejoinder:

> Would it surprise Sir Ralph Williams ... to know that there are in South Africa 600,000 half-castes who are offspring of white men and black women, and that a similar number of half-castes with like parentage are to be found scattered over the various West Indian islands? ... I might say that I am voicing the feeling of my own race when I declare that my whole mind revolts against the seduction of my women and girls by white men – young girls of 13 and 14 years of age are used to gratify the base lust of white seducers and are left with half-caste children on their hands to mourn the 'honour' of the civilized white man.

Those blacks who married the women whom they associated with were, Hercules thought, to be congratulated. Williams was libelling white women who could see beyond superficial skin differences. Hercules' letter concluded:

> ... shame upon Sir Ralph Williams and others of his kind, who, having earned a living in the lands of blacks, and who, having exploited them and experienced every kindness at their hands, and who are even now in the enjoyment of a pension which black men are contributing towards, still show such lamentable lack of decency as to

---

16. *The Times* (16 June 1919).

libel the very people through whom they are getting their daily bread.[17]

The question of sexual antipathy was also raised at a meeting in Hyde Park in a Manifesto produced by the Society of Peoples of African Origin. The Manifesto argued that the 'only thing that prevents the lives of coloured men in this country being a deadly monotonous hell is the sympathy of British women.' The writers of the Manifesto were concerned to emphasize that the blacks in Britain were loyal British subjects, entitled to respect for serving the Empire in its moment of need. The police, instead, capitulated to lawless forces, including,

> dangerous foreigners ... plotting the break up and downfall of the British Empire. ... They believe that if only they can stir up British men by showing up in the most disgusting fashion all intercourse between black men and white women, then they will be on a fair road to accomplishing their objects.[18]

Even if some blacks were insistent on their status as British subjects, several commentators were conscious of the fact that they were beginning to form distinct communities in the areas of their settlement. In Liverpool, nearly all blacks lived in the dockside areas in the South side of the city. The tendency to cluster in distinct neighbourhoods was thought by the editor of the *Liverpool Echo* to be more pronounced in the city than other cities in Britain. He distinguished 'Chinatown', 'dark-town' and

---

17. *The Times* (19 June 1919).
18. *Liverpool Courier* (16 June 1919).

'other alien quarters'. While in some respects an acceptable development (it allowed the authorities to overlook the doings of foreigners and provided a check against the pollution of a healthy community by undesirables), the editor thought it also produced a sense of special identity which excluded the whites and safeguarded 'the vicious elements' living among the mainly 'quiet and law abiding Negroes'.[19] Though stated in terms of the balance of advantage between alternative strategies of social control, the editor's musings presage the unresolved debate between those who on the one hand demanded assimilation and integration by immigrant communities into what was conceived in monopolistic terms as a single culture, and those who were prepared to accord a measure of cultural autonomy to a segment in what was seen as an increasingly ethnically heterogeneous and diverse society.

The third explanation we have identified is one that saw the riots purely in terms of hooliganism or manipulation by outside elements.[20] 'It was a convenient explanation for those who did not wish to grapple with more fundamental grievances, and one that, as we have seen above, the Society for the Peoples of African Origin was not above using itself.' By attributing the disturbances to the work of nefarious outsiders or the actions of deviant elements on either side, the widespread involvement by the white community and the wider repercussions of the disturbance on black communities in England and the colonies could be played down.

Finally, we turn to the question of employment. This factor was critically linked to the growth of an international division

---

19. *Liverpool Echo* (6 June 1919).
20. For one example, see *Liverpool Courier* (11 June 1919).

of labour based essentially on colour lines. A black sailor signed on at a colonial port could be paid at a rate much lower than those applying at any British port. This provoked white hostility by undercutting the rate for the job, and, on the other hand, encouraged black sailors to settle in Britain in the hope of obtaining better pay and conditions. As Richmond argues, the black sailor got the worst of both worlds: inferior pay if he signed on overseas, white retaliation if he tried to sign on in Britain.[21] The demands of the war-time economy led directly to an increase in the number of foreigners, both aliens and British subjects, in Liverpool. Workers were needed in the munitions and other factories, while many more served in the army and navy. The demobilization of this last group swelled the black population in Liverpool to about 5,000 persons, many of whom were in direct competition with a large number of English workers who had returned from the forces to the city demanding jobs.

The consequences were immediately deleterious to the black population as a whole. In several large factories, where blacks had worked for years, the refusal of white workers to work alongside blacks led to the dismissal of black labourers.[22] One local paper estimated that at the height of the riots 120 black workers had been dismissed for this reason.[23] Several specific cases can be cited to illustrate the pressures of job competition. One Nigerian, who worked for the shipping company, Elder Dempster, had a particularly unfortunate experience. Torpedoed in the Black Sea during the war, he returned to Liverpool only to find his possessions sold on the

---

21. Richmond, op. cit., 1955, p. 235.
22. *Liverpool Echo* (11 June 1919).
23. *Liverpool Courier* (11 June 1919).

assumption that he was dead. When he tried to sign up, he complained of being told: 'No colour. When white men finish you get job.' 'White men never finish', he lamented.[24]

In this and other cases, the attitudes of the unions and white workers, rather than the management, appear to have been decisive. The crews of the four Blue Funnel Line ships at Birkenhead refused to sail under a Chinaman as Chief Steward when there were 'thousands of Britishers wanting berths'.[25] Finally, we can cite the example of an Indian who had served four years in the Navy and then worked on a Mersey river hopper. He was fired at 24-hours' notice and told: 'You were quite efficient but there are 11,000 demobilized soldiers to be reinstated and they must have first chance.' He had searched for other posts but failed, even finding that Scandinavians were hired in preference to black labour: 'the white men must be reinstated first, the unions insist on it', he complained.[26]

We turn next to the role of the police, and the responses of the black community and the British authorities to the race riots. James Walvin argues that the handling of the riots by the police and the courts showed 'scandalously biased treatment' against the blacks. Many more blacks were arrested than whites and some were, according to a *Times* report quoted by Walvin, placed in an internment camp pending repatriation.[27] We were not able to find any other reference to internment, and it is likely that 'internment' referred either to the fact that police stations provided a refuge for blacks during the riots or that the setting up of internment camps was a proposal that was not in fact

---

24. *West Africa* (20 August 1921).
25. *Liverpool Courier* (11 June 1919).
26. Ibid.
27. Walvin, op. cit., p. 208.

implemented. In addition, one must offset against complaints of police discrimination, the statement by the Secretary of the Ethiopian Hall that 'we owe [the police] our lives'.[28] There is some evidence, too, that the police genuinely tried to break up the riots by increased recruitment and special patrols in the sensitive areas. On the other hand, as Walvin points out, local police initiative often had the effect of turning an administrative order against aliens into a racialist practice directed against blacks. As a result of the riots, the Superintending Officer at the port of Liverpool introduced a special registration card and finger print before aliens could be paid off or sign on a ship.[29] The scheme was thought so good that it was implemented at other ports and later given administrative sanction in the Aliens Order of 1925. Local police in Cardiff apparently took pains to register all 'coloureds' as aliens – thus making them subject to arbitrary deportation – despite the fact that the Order was not meant to apply to black British citizens.[30]

There was considerable ambivalence in the response of the black community to the race riots. Several who were established in the community were concerned to defend the image of the black man and to insist on their status as British subjects. 'We are not the rotters our detractors tried to make out. We are British and love Britain', said one petition.[31] Another proposal discussed at the time by some African merchants in Liverpool, was to spend £10,000 to 'erect a monument to the coloured people for the part they took in the war'.[32] Other blacks were

---

28. *West Africa* (13 September 1919).
29. Head Constable's Report (Liverpool) 1919.
30. Walvin, op. cit., p. 210.
31. *Liverpool Courier* (16 June 1919).
32. *Liverpool Daily Post* (11 June 1919).

more immediately concerned about the restriction on their employment opportunities and the problems of finding a berth to go back to their countries of origin. One coloured soldier wrote to the *Liverpool Daily Post*: 'Simply send us back to where your ships took us from ... and all you people who is out there making a living can come home and make their lives here.' 'We want to go back home', commented another, 'our position is such we are entitled to sympathy.'[33]

Such letters and expressions of opinion from black people reinforced a demand from several sections of white opinion for immediate repatriation. Discharged sailors' and soldiers' organizations in Liverpool appealed to the Lord Mayor to lend his voice to those demanding repatriation. Indeed, a couple of months prior to the riots, the Lord Mayor and the Secretary of the Ethiopian Hall discussed why in a scheme which offered 200 berths only 40 had been filled. This scheme was one amongst several that met with general failure. Reliable figures are hard to come by, but Walvin suggests only 627 had been repatriated by August 1921.

The reasons for the failure of repatriation are threefold. First, it appears that the demand for repatriation by blacks was exaggerated, either by wishful thinking on the part of the whites or by undue weight being lent to the views of a few black spokespeople. Certainly, the expectation by the *Liverpool Echo* that 'on the offer of a free passage or a small sum of money the majority will be willing to leave', was unfulfilled.[34] Next, it appears that the conditions of repatriation were unacceptable to many black sailors. Not surprisingly, many were resistant to the

---

33. Ibid; and *Liverpool Courier* (11 June 1919).
34. *Liverpool Echo* (17 June 1919).

idea of being unceremoniously shipped off and insisted on their right to be paid as full members of crew, provided with reasonable accommodation, and discharged in their ports of destination.

Finally, governmental action seems to have been inefficient or haphazard. The British government first tried to encourage the ship owners to employ as many black hands as possible on ships sailing to the West Indies or West Africa. This policy, as we have shown, met some resistance from white sailors wanting employment and relied, as the African chaplain to a hostel in Toxteth wrote, on private firms being prepared to shoulder a responsibility that was not essentially theirs.[35] When the government tried to deal directly with the question of repatriation, government departments tried to pass the buck. An official of the Home Office explained that law and order was a civic responsibility, while repatriation was difficult to cope with as the majority of blacks were British subjects. Things would have been much simpler had they been aliens, 'for there is a short and easy way of dealing with them'.[36] The Colonial Office argued that while they were ordinarily interested in the welfare of British subjects, they felt that as the matter had originated during the war it could more properly be dealt with by the war departments concerned (these departments included the War Department itself, the Labour Ministry, the Board of Trade and the Ministry of Shipping). Through this miasma of bureaucratic muddle, a clear policy for aliens did emerge. Many Chinese (excluding those who had established businesses in the country), and Norwegian, Danish and Swedish subjects,

---

35. *Liverpool Echo* (16 June 1919).
36. *Liverpool Courier* (12 June 1919).

brought to England to work in agriculture and the munitions factories, were deported.[37]

This hardly, however, touched the problem confronting unemployed blacks. As one example of a government-sponsored scheme we can cite the sailing of an Elder Dempster ship, the *Batanga*, for West Africa on 18 June 1919. The Home Office and the Ministry of Shipping, though noting that accommodation was for 240, thought 500 blacks might go if the facilities were adequate. Forty-three actually sailed from Liverpool, with another sixty joining the ship at Cardiff. The reasons adduced for the shortfall were that the notice of sailing was short and that some servicemen were awaiting war gratuities. Africans expressed their own views however: 'When we got on board [there was] nothing for sitting or sleeping for 250 for a 2–3 week voyage ... that's how the Ministry of Shipping rewards the Negro who has risked his lives for them during the war.'[38]

III

The fear that the Liverpool riots would have damaging effects in the Empire was expressed by several commentators in England. An editorial in the *Liverpool Daily Post*, for example, warned that:

> Careful and common-sense handling of the colour disturbances is necessary if what at present is little more than local hooliganism is not to develop into an Imperial problem. There would be unfortunate possibilities of

---

37. See *Liverpool Echo* (17 June 1919).
38. Letter in *Liverpool Echo* (20 June 1919).

mischief if any idea gained ground in India and Africa that the attitude of the [rioters] reflected British attitudes. ... This is, of course, to make the kind and generous treatment of the black races a matter of mere expediency. But such treatment is called for on the higher grounds of duty and justice.[39]

The Bishop of Liverpool also found that moral duty and self-interest were not incompatible. 'As members of the British Empire upon which the sun never sets, we are bound for our own welfare and the sake of our kith and kin to deal fairly and humanely with our fellow subjects.'[40] Sir Ralph Williams, in his letter cited earlier, surmised that every 'coloured newspaper' in the West Indies and West Africa would be seething with journalistic indignation at what they deemed the ill-treatment of their fellow-brethren.

Though clearly the Liverpool race riots were not directly connected with disturbances in other parts of the Empire, 1919 saw many protests against the colonial order. In India, constitutional agitation was followed by a massive strike in the Bombay cotton mills (involving 200,000 workers).[41] In

---

39. *Liverpool Daily Post* (11 June 1919).
40. *Liverpool Echo* (21 June 1919). It should perhaps be noted that Liverpool was the centre of 'reformist' Imperial thinking at the turn of the century associated with names like Mary Kingsley, E. D. Morel and John Holt. Sentiments concerning social justice in the Empire were probably more advanced there than elsewhere in England. For further information, see Kenneth Dike Nworah, 'The Liverpool "sect" and British West Africa: 1895–1915', *African Affairs* (vol. 70, 1971) pp. 349–64.
41. *Political Science Quarterly* (vol. 35, March 1920–December 1920) p. 104.

Chicago, Washington and New York, one of the first mass outbreaks of race riots in the Northern cities broke out in July 1919. In Chicago alone, thirty were killed and 500 wounded.[42] In South Africa, the African National Congress mounted a passive resistance campaign against the pass laws. Thousands threw away their passes and demanded to be arrested. The police obliged by arresting 700 and beating up, with the aid of white volunteers, scores of others.[43] Other disturbances took place in the Belgian Congo, in Egypt (where an insurrectionary movement started in March 1919) and in several other British colonies. In Belize (British Honduras), a riot in 1919 by black Hondurans was directed against a sudden increase in the prices charged by the white merchants. 'This is our country and we want to get the white man out. The white man has no right here', was a cry the rioters were heard to make.[44]

It was with some justice that socialist writers of the time invoked the spectres of the French revolution and the social discontent following the Napoleonic wars.[45] The sense of dissatisfaction with the Imperial order was both generalized and took specific forms in individual colonies. As one example, we may take the case of Sierra Leone on the West African coast. Here, in contrast to many other British colonies, the presence of a culturally anglophile group, the Creoles, might have been expected to cushion the impact of race consciousness.

---

42. See *West Africa* (9 August 1919) for speculation on the possible effects of this in West Africa.

43. H. J. and R. E. Simons, *Class and colour in South Africa 1850–1950* (Harmondsworth, 1969) pp. 221 and 222.

44. Robert G. Weisbord, 'Marcus Garvey, pan-Negroist: the view from Whitehall', *Race* (vol. 11, no. 4, April 1970) p. 420.

45. See, for example, Philip Snowden, *Labour and the new world* (London, n.d.).

However, strong protests were made by Creole elements about the colour-bar in appointments to the Civil Service, the lack of representative government and the big trade monopolies enjoyed by British firms.[46] Branches of the National Congress of British West Africa were organized in mid-1919 in Sierra Leone and the Gold Coast (Nigeria and the Gambia followed shortly thereafter), and, though composed of what by contemporary standards would be very straight-laced political figures, were accused of disloyalty against the British Empire and of making common cause with Sierra Leone's lumpen-proletariat![47]

The situation in Sierra Leone was complicated by the presence of numbers of Syrian and Lebanese small traders who bore the brunt of a more general dissatisfaction from several quarters with the running of the affairs of the colony. As J. Ayodele Langley writes:

> The frustration of the educated classes, the African trader and the unemployed in the big towns was given open expression in the rice and anti-Syrian riots of 1919 and in the workers' strike of the same year. Though directed against the Lebanese traders, these riots were in fact a violent and uncoordinated protest against what were believed to be injustices arising from the management of the colonial economy.[48]

---

46. See J. Ayodele Langley, *Pan-Africanism and nationalism in West Africa 1900–1945* (Oxford, 1973) p. 158.
47. Ibid, p. 163.
48. Ibid, pp. 199 and 200. For more on the strikes on the railway and the Public Works Department, see H. E. Conway, 'Labour protest activity in Sierra Leone', *Labour History* (no. 15, 1968) pp. 49–63.

The discharged sailors and soldiers were particularly outraged at the failure of the government to pay promised war gratuities. A petition organized by leading Creoles in the Colony at the time of the riots (which ironically broke out on 18 July 1919, the night of the celebrations held to mark the conclusion of the Peace Treaty) also indicated that the racial disturbances in England were not far from the minds of the rioters. According to petitioners, for a few weeks preceding the riots,

> there was considerable indignation in some parts of the city [Freetown] at the report of racial disturbances in Liverpool, Cardiff and a few other places in England and Wales which gave rise to considerable apprehension that the 'sea-boys' repatriated from those places with a deep sense of injury would instigate reprisals in Sierra Leone against the white residents.[49]

Money was actually collected in West Africa to repatriate the stranded African sailors.[50]

Few colonial authorities were prepared to seek the causes of these outbreaks in the exploitative relationship conditioned by the colonial experience and in the concomitant development of an international division of labour and occupation stratified basically along colour lines. They preferred instead to seek out the trouble in the work of outside agents. The Governor of Sierra Leone had 'some reason to believe' that money and organization from outside the Empire inspired the manifestations of disloyalty. Langley speculates that this could have

---

49. Cited in Langley, op. cit., p. 208.
50. Banton, op. cit., p. 35.

been a reference to either the Comintern or the Marcus Garvey's Universal Negro Improvement Association.[51] The Governor of Honduras thought that German, or German American, money or propaganda was behind the UNIA's activity in Belize.

That the British government was seriously concerned with the threat posed by the increase in racial consciousness can be shown by some fascinating correspondence originating from American State Department sources. One item in particular bears reproduction.[52] It was written from a Parisian hotel by one H. M. Worley, an American intelligence agent, to an assistant secretary at the State Department in Washington in August 1919. Worley was observing the Versailles conference and in particular the activities of the Pan-African and Liberian delegates. He refers at one point to a meeting with Sir Basil Thompson of Scotland Yard's Intelligence Service with respect to Social Unrest in the World.

> [Sir Basil] told me of the strikes and political disturbances in Sierra Leone, Jamaica and other British colonies where blacks far outnumber the whites. The British seem very apprehensive of a united movement on the part of the coloured race and are making special enquiries into any racial cohesion or unity among the coloured races generally.

---

51. Langley, op. cit., p. 42.
52. An exact reference to this document is difficult for us to give. It was consulted in an unclassified set of microfilms from the American National Archives lodged in the University of Liberia's library, Monrovia. It may be one of the documents referred to by Robert G. Weisbord (op. cit., p. 419, fn. 1).

Worley was able to reassure Sir Basil Thompson that Liberia was unlikely to be in the forefront of such unrest, but commented that 'wild rumours' had been circulating in France as to the magnitude of the race trouble in Washington, Chicago and New York. The Liberian *chargé* had apparently advised his President-Elect King (of Liberia) not to visit the US as thousands of blacks had been killed and the President would be insulted. (President King did in fact visit England, where, Worley claims, the British Monarch acted on advice that he should entertain the Head of State lavishly so as to demonstrate to his colonial subjects that a visiting black leader could be treated with due respect.) Worley's letter to Washington concluded by stating that it had been suggested both in France and England that the Japanese were inciting and financing the activities of radical blacks.

IV

We have attempted in this article to use some detailed data from our Liverpool case study to identify the links between the early manifestations of racial feeling in England and the contradictions inherent in the maintenance of the colonial order itself. If colonialism produced race consciousness, its continued survival was threatened by the retaliatory racial forces it released. The period immediately after the First World War was one which seriously threatened the maintenance of European hegemony. In several ways the period represented an aborted and uncoordinated mass revolt by colonial subjects. Consciousness of shared injustices for the most part became diverted into constitutional channels and demands for equal status and political rights. At an epiphenomenal level, some images of this period survived. One researcher, for example, found that in the parallel case of Cardiff, the violent clashes after the First World War, survived as bitter folk-memories in the late 1960s.[53] But, at a structural level, the contemporary relevance of our data should be apparent. Racism in Britain is deeply rooted in the mode of domination cemented by the Imperial heritage. The disappearance of racial discrimination in Britain may not follow simply or automatically from a dramatic overturning of the relationships of dominance and disability between black and white on a world-wide scale. Equally, however, racism in one country cannot disappear without black liberation everywhere.

---

53. L. Bloom, Introduction to K. Little, op. cit., 1972, p. 39.

9. Fifty Years of Labour Studies

Josh DeWind

 Half a century is a long time. It is long enough to experience and try to make sense of major social transformations. By examining the international framework that informed Robin's earlier works (*Peasants and proletarians* and *The new helots*) and his later works (*Migration and its enemies* and *Global sociology*), I shall try to capture the ways in which Robin's scholarship on labour and the world has evolved in tandem. A constant throughout has been Robin's capacious intellect – one that is inclusive and seeks to bring all people in under his tent.

Intellectually, Robin has sought to understand and explain how all people in the world are interconnected – in our age through the voracious spread of capitalist relations of production and consumption. Morally – growing up after the holocaust and in apartheid South Africa – Robin's scholarly work has pursued an imperative to break the cages of persecution, exclusion and inequality that divide humanity.

Robin is a universalist whose intellect and moral reach has found a place for us all in his broad overview, one that has given greater meaning to our own lives. This is what I heard from others yesterday and, at any rate, has certainly been true for me. *Peasants and proletarians* includes two articles that I wrote about peasants and landless workers in Peru and Jamaica who become wage labourers in the mines of Peru and sugar cane fields of Florida. This summer *Global Networks* published the results of a project that I have coordinated for the past ten years on *The religious lives of migrant minorities*. In both instances, the book and journal that have framed those publications have given them a wider import than I myself could have imagined but that Robin framed, intellectually and morally.

Let me summarize what I see to be the organizing principles of Robin's evolving intellectual and moral framework from:

- Marxism and Internationalism to
- Globalization and Cosmopolitanism

Marxism and internationalism

Peasants and proletarians presents us with a Marxist ideology into which Robin sough to show how the Third World of peasant and proletarian workers fits. In the opening sentences, he contrives unconvincingly to bring in Marx's views, rationalizing that it is because Marx's birthday is only three years away saying, 'one is jarred because many of Marx's views seem to be both startlingly relevant and even contemporaneous.'[1] He concludes that capitalism has fragmented the working class, including all peasants and proletarians, and asks the central question that preoccupies him: 'are we to witness the collapse of

---

1. Robin Cohen, Peter C. W. Gutkind and Phyllis Brazier (eds) *Peasants and proletarians: the struggles of third world workers* (New York: Monthly Review Press, 1979) p. 9.

proletarian international internationalism? ... Or are metropolitan workers going to establish bonds of solidarity with migrants at home and their brothers abroad so as to match the flexibility and adaptability of transnational capital?'[2]

What is 'jarring' to me today is not the relevance of Marx's thought but the seemingly ideological formulation of Marxist rhetoric. But what is ideology? One version might be that ideology is the formulation of a truth or a version of the truth that if adopted by a social movement will enable its adherents to change the world for the better. Some ideologies are more inclusive and human than others: the exclusionary and murderous fundamentalism of the Islamic State is horrifying but the universalism of human rights is less so. Was Robin a Marxist ideologue? *The new helots* confirms that he was not.

In fact, in that book Robin developed a fundamental critique that built upon but also challenged Marx's view of capitalism as a mode of production based simply on the relation of capital to free wage labour. The book argues that historically capitalism expanded through the coercive incorporation of labourers engaged in non-capitalist modes of production – the peasants as well as the proletarians of both the core and periphery. In Robin's view, regional political economies extended globally through mercantile, industrial, financial and global phases of capitalist development to incorporate workers based in non-capitalist social formations.

In sum, Robin's framework was that of an internationalist who sought to use his scholarship to find a way forward for the anti-capitalist struggle by showing how workers of the world really are brought together, if not yet united, by capitalism.

---

2. Ibid., p. 23.

Would the 'new internationalism' succeed in uniting workers of the world to overthrow the coercive nature of capitalism? Thus far – and we have seen and supported half a century of transformative struggle – the answer has been 'no'?

The socialist states that gave material and social credibility to a Marxist analysis have collapsed and taken a national capitalist road in the cases of both the USSR and China. Cuba ceases to export revolution, while the struggles for national liberation in Africa and Asia have foundered on the rocks of nationalist capitalism. Under the banner of neo-liberalism, capitalism has fostered a remarkably intensive and extensive process of globalization.

Globalization and cosmopolitanism

One indication of how Robin's intellectual and moral frameworks have evolved can be found by examining his critique of the alternative view of the new international division of labour. In *The new helots* (1987) Robin explained how he preferred an alternative model he had developed in the book, 'namely that capitalism has been characterized by a combination of unfree and free labour regimes from its genesis to the present day … in each phase a mix of "free" and "unfree" labour forms is evident. Equally, the hoary contest between capital and labour ever takes place.'[3]

Two decades later, in *Migration and its enemies* (2006), Robin's critique of NIDL replaces his earlier 'preferred view' of worker internationalism with a chapter on 'globalization'. The growth of this mundane or everyday cosmopolitanism has profound implications, though we should be cautious about

---

3. Robin Cohen, *The new helots: migrants in the international division of labour* (Aldershot: Avebury/Gower Publishing Group, 1987) p. 252.

exaggerating its political significance. The new army of global migrants is not the conscious, politicized international working class that Marx imagined in the 1848 *Communist manifesto*. Nonetheless, there is a sense in which 'globalization from above, driven by powerful countries and transnational corporations, is now being paralleled and to a degree subverted by "globalization from below", driven by the enhanced mobility of labour.'[4]

In *Global sociology*, written in partnership with Paul Kennedy, their critique of the new international division of labour is presented in the context of a discussion of uneven development. They argue that the logic of accumulation that drives the world capitalist system has developed some regions and social sectors and underdeveloped others and it has created severe crises that create uncertainty about the global future of humanity. Reflecting perhaps Marx's analytic concept of dialectical materialism, they argue that at the same time capitalist globalization has also created the technologies and social relations of production and consumption that foster opportunities for global civil society and global social movements that have the potential to address these crises.

Although they point out that workers' movements are still active in emerging economies such as China, Brazil, India and Nigeria,[5] their analysis suggests that the international labour movement's revolutionary potential has been replaced by global peace, human rights, women's, environmental and other global social movements.

---

4. Robin Cohen, *Migration and its enemies: global capital, migrant labour and the nation-state* (Aldershot: Ashgate, 2006) p. 192.
5. Robin Cohen and Paul Kennedy, *Global sociology* (Basingstoke: Palgrave Macmillan, 2013) p. 345.

Some global changes are very positive. They provide a greater potential than ever before for the world's inhabitants to forge new understandings, alliances and structures – both from below and in alliance with elite institutions – in the pursuit of more harmonious, environmentally sustainable and humanitarian solutions to local and global problems. ... The future directions of global society depend on us as ordinary world citizens, on what moral positions we choose and what battles we are prepared to fight. ... The key social challenge of the twenty-first century is to prise open the bars for these disadvantaged people so that they can discover the transformatory possibilities that globalization has generated.[6]

If so, then over the past 50 years the world has undergone intensive and extensive globalization and Robin's intellectual and moral framework has evolved in tandem from 'workers of the world unite' under the banner of internationalism to 'movements of the world unite' under the banner of cosmopolitanism. Under that banner we all have important roles to play whether as workers or intellectuals.

---

6. Ibid., pp. 406–7.

10. Robin Cohen and Nigerian Labour Studies: An Intellectual Appreciation

Jimi O. Adesina

The encounters with Professor Robin Cohen would be, for many, diverse and varied. For me they are both intellectual and personal. The intellectual was in a threefold movement: first, being keenly aware of his works, then becoming a doctoral supervisee, and then an enduring engagement with his works. The personal started as the intellectual and deepened with time. Robin Cohen supervised my doctoral thesis at the University of Warwick. Going to Warwick was something I did with considerable reluctance, I should say. I had applied for a place at Oxford and had received a direct D.Phil. admission to study at St Peter's College (with Gavin Williams and Eric Batstone at Templeton College). The coup of December 1983 had delayed the final release of my Nigerian federal government scholarship, but I had also applied for the

Commonwealth Scholarship. When the Commonwealth Scholarship Commission finally came back to me, it was to the effect, as its letter stated, that concerning the course for which I had applied, Warwick University 'is to be preferred'. The Commonwealth Scholarship, I was informed in no uncertain terms, would be tenable only at Warwick. With barely a month to my expected resumption date at either Warwick or Oxford and no end in sight to the embargo on new financial outlay by the new military regime in 1984, I caved in and packed my bags for Warwick. Whatever my initial anger at the Commonwealth Scholarship Commission, forcing me to go to Warwick is by far the best decision anyone has ever made on my behalf or imposed on me. It was a case of someone shaving my head in my absence, as the Yoruba saying would put it.

What made Warwick such a great experience was that I had the good fortune of having as my thesis supervisors two of the most wonderful human beings under whom anyone could ever work. One is Richard Hyman; the other is Robin Cohen. That forced migration set the stage for a sustained engagement over three years with Robin Cohen and an incredible doctoral education that morphed into an enduring bond with a mentor, a remarkable friend and constant facilitator – someone who always 'had my back'. With Robin and Selina Cohen one could depend on generous and open hearts and a home to rest your weary bones, but I shall return to that later.

I shall now focus on Robin's contribution to Nigerian labour studies and use his work to counter some current trends in African studies. I ask what has gone wrong with the Africanists' preoccupation with Africa compared with the scholarship that Robin and many of his generation represent.

Robin Cohen's paper on 'Resistance and Hidden Forms of

Consciousness among African Workers' has been mentioned several times (see http://www.roape.org/pdf/1902.pdf). I will return to an aspect of Robin's 'hidden forms' to the study of Africa in the final section.

The study of Africa or African studies?

At two levels, I need to declare my personal antipathy to something called 'African Studies'. This is partly because I consider quite problematic the idea of someone spending a few months in a country on a specific topic turning round to claim *expertise* on anything African.

It is also partly because my own disciplinary sensibilities tell me that even as an African (a Nigerian by birth and a South African by domicile), I cannot claim expertise on everything Nigerian or South African. Only in the context of interpreting a 'foreign world and strange people' to one's own fellow nationals would the ability to speak a few words in a 'native' tongue translate into privileged access to the inscrutable minds and knowledge of the natives.

In this regard, I would like to make a distinction between 'the study of Africa' and 'African studies'. Once these caveats are taken, I believe that an assessment of the applicable parts of Cohen's works becomes easier to undertake and stand in sharp contrast to the return to native gazing that has increasingly marked the African segment of areas studies.

Here I return to my first encounter with Robin Cohen because, although the physical encounter was in October 1984, the intellectual encounter happened a few years before then. Here we turn to *Labour and politics in Nigeria*.[1]

---

1. R. Cohen, *Labour and politics in Nigeria 1945–1971* (London: Heinemann, 1974).

Labour and politics in Nigeria (1945–1971)

Labour and politics in Nigeria was published in 1974; it was the outcome of research undertaken between 1967 and 1969 for his Ph.D. thesis at the University of Birmingham (under the supervision of Ken Post and Arnold Hughes). During the period of the thesis research, Robin Cohen was affiliated to the Department of Political Science, at the University of Ibadan. He updated the data for the book during a visit to Nigeria in late 1971/early 1972.[2] My own encounter with the book was at graduate school in Ibadan while I was doing my master's degree in industrial and labour relations at the Department of Sociology. I had done my undergraduate work in the Department of Political Science – with sociology and economics as some of my 'electives' – and would start my university career in the same university 13 years after Robin and Selina left Ibadan.

My fascination in graduate school with *Labour and politics* was at several levels. I remember being particularly impressed by two things. The first is the rich data and attention to detail that underpin the analysis in the work. This is all the more remarkable considering that the bulk of the fieldwork was done during the difficult period of the Nigerian civil war. Second is the preference for nuanced analysis. Robin's normative commitment was without doubt to me as a reader, but I got the constant feeling reading the book that it is a case of ideological commitment *not* getting in the way of scholarship. I will return to this as an important difference with the dominant trend in contemporary Africanist discourse of Africa. In the light of contemporary studies of Africa by a new crop of 'specialists', there is a third aspect of *Labour and politics* (and all of Robin's

---

2. R. Cohen, *Labour and politics in Nigeria 1945–1971* (London: Heinemann, 1974) p. vi.

works as far as I can discern) that is worth flagging – this is the extent to which Robin's works embrace and celebrate African agency and scholarship.

Labour and politics, as I noted, fascinated me as a graduate student in Ibadan, and here I will point to some of the dimensions of the book. First, the fine-grained attention to densely compacted data – deploying a range of research techniques – is evident across much of Robin's work and was something to which I could relate at graduate school in Ibadan.

Second, in a context in which everyone took it for granted that one could understand Nigeria and all things Nigerian in ethnic terms, Robin's discussion of trade unions was not simply about pushing a class line; it entailed a finely-grained multi-level effort to understand the nature of workers' organizations, unionism and union involvement in the politics of the country. He offered a micro, meso and macro-level appreciation of union dynamics. While individual workers may hold a range of identities, their formal organization in unions was anything but ethnic. Some of the unions were regionally based, which may reflect the boundaries of political structuring in the country, but that is not necessarily ethnic. I think that a further disaggregation that is warranted in the book is the distinction made between trade unions and trades associations. Many of the latter, including the associations of bricklayers, timber millers and vulcanizers, would often would register under the Trade Unions Ordinance although they were not formally trade unions.

Third, Robin addressed the Nigerian labour movement and the extent to which the notion of collective bargaining was a default mechanism for advancing workers' interests in the context of debunking the idea that political and economic unionism were pitted against one another. More than this, Robin's analysis shows that resorting to protests, mass rallies and general strike action is situational to contexts where collective bargaining is hardly appropriate when there is a massive power imbalance between workers and employers. His was not simply a situational analysis that confronts theory with data, but one that proceeds from an empathetic engagement with the workers' position in the employment environment and the broader political economy of a country. In other words, rather than seeing pathologies, he engages with the agency of the workers and the unions.

Fourth, it is perhaps with works like 'Resistance and hidden forms of consciousness'[3] that embracing the agency of the research subjects allows for situational analysis rather than turning the unfamiliar into pathologies. Examples he uses include Mauritian sugar-cane workers who had just been laid off setting fire to the sugar-cane plantation, or PWD workers smoking joints of marijuana in Mokola (Ibadan – Robin's 1968 field notes). His engagement with social action from the perspective of the agents themselves (rather than through stylized notions of appropriate behaviour signifying modernity or rational social order), allowed him to make important contributions to a broader body of scholarship beyond Africa. Hidden forms of resistance would become important in the labour process literature in the 1980s. The idea that insights derived from the study of Africa could form the basis of significant scholarship elsewhere is something that transverses all of Robin's work – from the understanding of class, class

---

3. Robin Cohen, 'Resistance and hidden forms of consciousness amongst African workers', *Review of African Political Economy*, vol. 19, 1980, pp. 8–22 (available at http://www.roape.org/pdf/1902.pdf).

formations, class consciousness, to issues of identity, migration and so on. In other words, the study of Africa and not simply the premise for writing onto Africa but of Africa speaking back, with distinct theoretical (or epistemic) significance. The sense I got of him is of a scholar genuinely fascinated by (and with an abiding curiosity about) the world of real human existence, and of one who is happy to embrace this conceptually.

Fifth, what remains a constant fascination (and a validation of the earlier influences on me at Ibadan of Omafume Onoge and John Ohiorhenuan) was that it is possible to be 'Marxist' without being doctrinaire. In many ways, this involved Robin confronting received conceptual Left dicta with his African field data to produce a more nuanced analysis that sometimes debunked and always refined the analysis. It was the same sense of liberation one found in Amilcar Cabral's seminal assertion about what immanent classes and class struggle mean to human history. In the face of the claim that 'the history of all hitherto existing societies is the history of class struggle',[4] Cabral[5] asks:

> Does history begin only with the development of the phenomenon of 'class', and consequently of class struggle? To reply in the affirmative would be to place outside history the whole period of life of human groups from the discovery of hunting, and later of nomadic and sedentary agriculture, to the organization of herds and the

---

4. Karl Marx and Frederich Engel, *Manifesto of the Communist Party* (London: Pluto Press, 1995) first published 1888.
5. Amilcar Cabral, 'The weapon of theory', address delivered to the first Tricontinental Conference of the Peoples of Asia, Africa and Latin America held in Havana in January 1966. www.marxists.org/subject/africa/cabral/1966/weapon-theory.htm.

private appropriation of land. It would also be to consider – and this we refuse to accept – that various human groups in Africa, Asia, and Latin America were living without history, or outside history, at the time when they were subjected to the yoke of imperialism. It would be to consider that the peoples of our countries, such as the Balantes of Guinea, the Coaniamas of Angola and the Macondes of Mozambique, are still living today – if we abstract the slight influence of colonialism to which they have been subjected – outside history, or that they have no history.

Cabral insists that the refutation is grounded 'on concrete knowledge of the socio-economic reality of our countries'. For Cabral, as for Robin, Omafume Onoge, John Ohiorhenuan, Ifi Amadiume or Archie Mafejé, the significance of being true to one's ethnographic data is never to be afraid of which sacred chicken's feathers will end up being truly plucked.

Sixth, the concept of 'elite' both as a pejorative term in the study of Africa, and as a binary contrasting of 'elite' and the 'masses', is an issue that Robin addressed in the 1972 *Socialist Register* article 'Class in Africa'.[6]

Far from there being any serious attention given to the structural consequences of … economic developments, the subtlety and complexity of social relationships has usually being downgraded by the adoption of the simple

---

6. Robin Cohen, 'Class in Africa: analytical problems and perspectives', *Socialist Register*, vol. 9, 1972, pp. 231–55 (available free at http://socialistregister.com/index.php/srv/article/view/5312#.Vq4-hFnpWg1).

expedient of contraposing the terms 'elite' and 'mass' to delineate salient social divisions.[7]

The 'elite' and 'masses' sometimes become entangled in an invidious but mutually beneficial relationship, which is something that the 'neo-patrimonialism' school embraced with some enthusiasm. Anyway, apropos this, quite early on Robin warned that 'the accumulated evidence of popular dissatisfaction (in the form of tax riots, general strikes and rebellions) can hardly be thought of as exhibiting acquiescence, let alone deference to the pretensions of the independence leadership.'[8] Privileging the autonomy of political action among ordinary people, especially workers, is a recurring theme in much of Robin's work on Africa in general, but particularly Nigeria. He was also one of the first to rebut Arrighi and Saul's rigid demarcation of the African working class into a semi-proletarianized lower stratum and an upper stratum they claimed constituted a 'labour aristocracy' and part of the 'elite'.[9] In the face of an often formulaic transposition of class categories, Robin sought to offer a more nuanced view of the emergent class forces and multiple fault lines that shape and define social (and political) action. His focus on 'the political, intendant and working classes', as he himself admitted, is not because these are the most significant but because they are 'the most visible and permanent classes'.[10]

---

7. Cohen 1972, pp. 241–2.
8. Cohen 1972, p. 242.
9. G. Arrighi and J. S. Saul, 'Nationalism and revolution in sub-Saharan Africa', in R. Miliband and J. Saville (eds) *The socialist register* (London: Merlin Press, 1969).
10. Cohen 1972, p. 252.

One corrective I would like to enter relates to making sense of pre-1964 politics in Nigeria. Many of the analyses of politics in this period – including Ruth First's *Barrel of the gun*,[11] Ken Post[12] and others – pay insufficient attention to understanding the political dynamics in ideological terms. One needs to analyse the split within the Action Group, for instance, in ideological terms rather than simply through questions of corruption or jockeying for access to the largess of office that may flow from participating in the Federal government and cabinet in the period after independence. While it has had people who profess Marxist ideological preferences in its ranks and (through its media outlets and summer school for training cadres) has articulated these ideas in Action Group structures,[13] the party's decided shift to the left was increasingly articulated in its official party positions and statements by its party leader, Obafemi Awolowo. The party explicitly articulated 'democratic socialism' in its 1959 Federal elections manifesto and in 1960 presented it as the blueprint for post-independence Nigeria.[14] In a public lecture on 27 January 1961, the party leader articulated the case not only for democratic socialism but also for a radical

---

11. Ruth First, *The barrel of a gun: political power in Africa and the coup d'état* (Harmondsworth: Penguin, 1970).

12. Ken Post and Michael Vickers, *Structure and conflict in Nigeria, 1960–1965* (London: Heinemann Educational, 1973); Ken Post and George Jenkins, *The price of liberty: personality and politics in colonial Nigeria* (Cambridge: Cambridge University Press, 1973).

13. John A. A. Ayoade, 'Party and ideology in Nigeria: a case study of the Action Group', *Journal of Black Studies*, vol. 16, no. 2, 1985, pp.169–88.

14. Action Group, *Democratic socialism: being the manifesto of the Action Group of Nigeria for an independent Nigeria* (Ibadan: Ibadan African Press, 1960).

pan-Africanist vision that was close to Nkrumah's orientation.[15] In addition to insisting on welfare policies on education, healthcare, housing, a minimum wage and social insurance schemes, 'specifically old age pension [to] be paid to persons above a particular age', the economic policies involved 'the state [entering] many sectors of the national economy now held by foreign investors', and taking hold of the 'commanding heights' of the economy. It was also a vision that sought to advance the interests of Nigerian business people *vis-à-vis* foreign investors, but with restraints from the state to avoid the 'huge concentration of capital in a few hands'. The pan-African vision articulated in the lecture includes:

- the termination of colonial rule across the whole continent and all military pacts with foreign powers;
- 'the promotion of a community of interests among all the peoples of Africa and the eventual establishment of a political union or confederacy ... among African states'; and
- 'the mobilization of all our forces ... in the immediate extermination of apartheid in South Africa and the restoration to the African of his[or her] natural birth-rights'.

The position of the Action Group could not be more starkly at odds with the conservative orientation of the Federal government described 'at home' as an 'ideological orientation [of] *laissez faire* capitalism, and in the external sphere ... [as] subservience to the Western Bloc'.

New materials that have emerged suggest that the British, for

---

15. Obafemi Awolowo, 'Case for ideological orientation', a lecture given at the Adventist College of West Africa, Ilishan-Remo on 27 January 1961.

instance, took seriously the more ideological shift further to the left in the Action Group.[16] Clearly, in the post-Jos convention of the party, the Ladoke Akintola faction of the Action Group took seriously the idea of (democratic) socialism – a breakup that would eventually lead to the generalized political crisis in the Western Region and the formation of the Nigerian National Democratic Party[17] under the leadership of Ladoke Akintola. The campaigning by the Akintola faction against the idea of socialism suggests that they regarded the ideological dimension as equally important.

Pavement ethnography and gossip as scholarship

Against the grain of what the scholarship of Robin and many (though not all or even most) of his generation involved, the current state of Africanist writing has become increasingly defined by what I refer to as 'pavement ethnography' and confusing gossip. The mode of writing on Africa that has become increasingly popular in the wake of neoliberal conservatism and

---

16. BBC Radio 4, Monday, 30 July 2007 edition of Document, titled 'Rigging Nigeria', suggests that the fear of a left-wing ('communist') shift in Nigeria sufficiently preoccupied the British colonial administration for it to rig the 1959 Federal elections (www.bbc.co.uk/radio 4/history/document/document_20070730.shtml). The outcome of the elections resulted in a governing coalition of the Northern People's Congress (based in the Northern Region) and the National Council of Nigerian Citizens (NCNC, formerly National Council of Nigeria and the Cameroons), with the Action Group becoming the main opposition party. We may have to await the declassification of files, which Document could not obtain, to substantiate the claims that in relation to the Action Group, the British became increasingly agitated about having 'a second Nkrumah in West Africa'.
17. Not to be confused with a party of the same name established by Herbert Macaulay in 1923.

the postmodern reduction of everything to social construction has seen the deployment of 'evidence' used in the native gazing that privileges market mammy or beer parlour narratives. It is easy to report gossip, fail to provide an evidential basis for such gossip and yet be published. It is as if one could do a study of 1980s British politics by relying on what London cab drivers tell you about or the IRA, without testing such stories. These increasingly ahistorical analyses and a tendency to endogenize every crisis stand in sharp contrast to the capacity of this earlier generation. In their approach to political economy, these scholars seemed able to locate the local within global economic and power dynamics. Finally, the complete evacuation of African agency stands in sharp contrast to the earlier generation that took seriously not only African existential agency but also scholarship. Many of these works have coalesced around the 'Neopatrimonialism School' and have come to be its hallmark. On the grounds of its methodological, evidential and heuristic value, Mustapha[18] a while ago, and Mkandawire,[19] more recently, have offered a very comprehensive critique.

Again, I would like to make a distinction between African Studies and the study of Africa and reiterate that scholars from outside the continent of Africa, who are qualified to study Africa, are continuing to do a considerable amount of work on Africa. Their hallmark includes taking African data seriously

---

18. Abdul Raufu Mustapha, 'States, predation and violence: reconceptualizing political action and political community in Africa', paper presented at the 10th General Assembly of the Council for the Development of Social Science Research in Africa, Kampala, Uganda, 8–12 December 2002.
19. Thandika Mkandawire, 'Neopatrimonialism and the political economy of economic performance in Africa: critical reflections', *World Politic*, vol. 67, no. 3, 2015, pp. 563–612.

without resorting to what Michael Chege called 'brazen name calling', paying due regard to the agency of Africans and locating the local within the wider global matrix of power and privilege. In these and many other ways Robin's scholarly works on Nigeria specifically (especially its labour movements) and Africa more generally are a fine example to succeeding generations of how to approach and analyse the continent.

Hidden forms of contribution to the study of Africa: in lieu of a conclusion

I should not end without highlighting what I call Robin's 'hidden forms of contribution' to the study of Africa, and here I return to the personal, drawing on my experience of his and Richard Hyman's supervision. Having a supervisor who is friend, mentor and thesis guide is probably the best wish of any thesis candidate. In my case, both Richard and Robin trusted me sufficiently to give me the space to develop my ideas and for a thesis that seemed determined to be meta-theoretical to proceed without letting go of my hands. When, after months of writing up, I got to the point where I thought I needed to return to the library for further reading – I needed to crack the idea of abstract labour sociologically – they gave me the space. It meant I overshot my scholarship funding by three months, but I could come back to them with a thesis I felt (at least for that time) represented the best effort I could muster at the time. It is a lesson in supervision that I have carried with me since.

There is a subsidiary aspect to this story. Ibadan was a place of highbrow scholarship – literally. You sat in seminars with your eyebrows knotted up in the high position because you were trying to figure out what 'Stakhanovite tradition' or 'imperialist cartography' meant. If there is one thing I learnt from Robin and

Richard, it was that scholarship is first about communication. As the music teacher, Benjamin Shorofsky, told his Italian protégé, Bruno Martelli, in an edition of the 1980s television series, *Fame,* 'the first musician was not the virtuoso who played in the cave, but the one who came out of the cave to play to an audience.' The idea that mutual unintelligibility could be regarded as a mark of scholarship was something that Richard and Robin disabused without often stating it as such. They led through the examples of their own scholarly work. If the postmodern drivel did not gain traction with me, it is partly because of my experience with Robin and Richard at Warwick.

Since my Warwick days Robin has remained a friend, mentor and facilitator. When I left Oxford at the end of my sabbatical year in 2008, Robin bequeathed me his South African library. Before and after, I always felt welcome in Robin and Selina's home whatever the time of the day.

To Robin and Selina, I would like to end by saying 'thank you.'

11. Reflections on Globalization: Before and After

Paul Kennedy

In the beginning

Robin had already planned the outline of our jointly authored book, *Global Sociology*, in some detail and sold its possibilities to Macmillan before I came on the scene. In 1995 he generously invited me to become a joint author and we began thinking about the overall architecture of the book and what could and/or should be the priority themes, questions and case studies to include in the writing.

I think from the outset that we both thought about globalization as a definite and important set of processes and transformations that had become ever more evident at all levels of human interaction – pressing on governments, peoples, cultures and, in geographical or spatial terms, continents, nations, regions and localities – and that they were set to continue in this way. We were confident that these changes needed to be given a sharper conceptual identity and focus, which until then most social scientists (with significant exceptions like Robertson,

Axford and Albrow) lacked. We also felt that their multiple impacts on every kind of human experience could and should be highlighted. In particular, they needed to be brought to the attention of sociologists and other social scientists and placed fully under the sociological spotlight. Indeed, we saw it as a challenge to play our part in encouraging the discipline not to abandon the national/societal frame of reference that had dominated the subject until then, but to nudge sociology into acknowledging and incorporating global processes into the curriculum.

Certainly, we saw globalization penetrating all socio-cultural spheres. However, we needed to take into account centuries of modernity, capitalism, international relations and the legacy of imperialism, not to mention the power and resilience of various ethnic, religious, local and national affiliations and loyalties. Since all these were grounded in ongoing sets of daily social relations everywhere, they remained extremely powerful and more often than not would prove capable of resisting, absorbing or modifying globalizing forces. Thus, globalization and the local were set to interact and feed off each other in ways that would only become clear over time. The sphere of the glocal, as Robertson suggested, required a good deal of careful conceptualization and was where everything was happening and would happen. Nothing could be assumed or prejudged concerning how global–local processes might pan out. As Robin so pertinently said in a recent interview for the journal *Critical Globalization Studies*, we have been less interested in producing a sociology of globalization than a sociology that takes account of and brings the global into the centre of sociological analysis – a global sociology.

I cannot speak for Robin, but for me and my thoughts on

national and world prospects, the mid to late 1990s was a heady period. I think there was an optimism in the air, not least the real prospect of an end to years of Conservative government in the UK and the imposition of New Labour policies on the British people and economy. Recall the following:

- an era of world capitalist growth – expanding trade flows, stock market ebullience until the dotcom crash, rising incomes for many people in the West, improved employment prospects for most, relatively high economic growth in the USA towards the end of the Clinton era and America's huge national debt being reduced;
- daily news of China's astonishing economic growth pulling millions out of poverty and demonstrating the largest rural–urban migration in history. There was also revival and growth in Latin America after the two decades of economic stagnation in the 1970s and 1980s; India was at last escaping from years of abject poverty; and Mandela had become South Africa's president;
- EU integration was proceeding and there were ever larger numbers of students on Erasmus programmes, plus electoral majorities in favour of EU integration – ever greater flows of professionals were moving across national boundaries and working for global companies and engendering cosmopolitanism;
- there was the end of the Cold War and victory for capitalist democracy – the former USSR and its satellites were opening up rapidly to Western business and market influences. Fukuyama also predicted the 'end of history', though I suspect that few of us took his arguments seriously;
- a few Islamicist-fuelled terrorist events had occurred, but

nothing on the scale of either 9/11 in 2001 or all that followed in terms of neo-Conservative military reaction in the Middle East, which dominated much of the world political situation in the noughties.

Nearly everything in the news and much of what academics were writing seemed optimistic about the future. A world was opening up to other views and cultures, a world of increasing mobility, peaceful mass migration, genuine multicultural cities and of networking possibilities on a scale never before seen or thought possible. There were new Internet-based forms of communication; we were going to see new forms of political protest, which IT supported transnational links, as with Mexico's Zapatistas, would invigorate. TNCs were bringing jobs and investment to previously remote regions and tying the workers and consumers of the world together through endless global supply chains that might be exploitative, but at least linked countries to some form of economic interdependence. Interconnectivity was the buzzword and interdependency was ever more entangling the lives of the world's people.

For me, all this pointed to two major possibilities:

First, there was the real prospect that these interconnectivities would allow the dispossessed, the radical and the exploited worldwide to join together to overcome oppression and injustice to an extent never before possible.

Second, there was the prospect that interconnectivity would raise most people's awareness of the commonality of problems worldwide – climate change, poverty, inequality, the dangers of unregulated capitalist markets, transnational crime and terrorism, US neoconservatism, imperialism and the need to sink cultural and political differences in the search for cooperative solutions.

After 2000: the reckoning

Robin, I think, may have been less taken in by these possibilities, but even he, I suspect, did not escape some of this feeling of optimism. This was the sense that the *Global sociology* project was more than just another student textbook and that it might contribute in some way to opening people's eyes to the need to join in the many worldwide struggles for social justice. I believe that even a brief review of *Global sociology 1* bears out my argument that enthusiasm for the positive potential of globalization was clearly evident in many of its chapters (for example in the final chapter of *Global sociology 1*, which Robin wrote). Moreover, this same orientation and conviction is evident in *Global sociology 2* published in 2007, although in a more subdued form and even though by this time the world looked very different from the possibilities and promise of the late 1990s. However, *Global sociology 3* is, I suggest, much more circumspect in its analysis, more critical of globalization processes *per se*, more certain that older structures, cultures, relationships and forms of oppression across the world – linked both to tradition and modernity – are surviving, proving resistant to the pressure of globalizing forces. So what explains this greater caution, circumspection – the transition from definite optimism about the potential of globalization for contributing to 'positive' changes, to an understanding that, if anything, it veers more towards pessimism?

There are several possible explanations but I would like briefly to outline four. We can argue about what might constitute the quintessential core experiences that globalization

brings but we probably will not go far wrong if we state something along the following lines:

- a sense of relative deterritorialization – the sense that we can
  no longer explain our lives solely in terms of national/ local
  factors and processes: that, instead, our lives are criss-
  crossed by and tied into events and people far away – we have
  been lifted out of the normal and the local. This brings
  advantages and excitement but also anxiety as we are no
  longer able so readily to make sense of our lives – a feeling
  of disorientation, even a sense of 'invasion';
- the awareness that we no longer live in cultural isolation but
  are continuously exposed to multiple cultural fragments
  coming from 'outside' – whether in terms of music, cuisine,
  costume, family customs, religious beliefs, the obligation of
  public life, interpretations of history and so on. Again, this is
  simultaneously exciting and provocative but also threatening
  and confusing – especially for the less educated and those
  who need their sense of 'order' and certainty because their
  lives are uncertain and filled with insecurity;
- sociality at all scales of existence becomes more shaped by
  and dependent on networking – it consists of loose, open
  (stretching in all directions and 'out' into global social space),
  borderless and, sometimes, semi-incoherent forms of
  relationships. They bring greater opportunities and forms of
  attachment, but at the same time they also perhaps bring
  more choices, a greater 'thinness' to our relationships and
  more uncertainties than we can always bear. Perhaps we long
  for a more compact, dense, reliable and bordered social life;
- the sheer growing complexity of every aspect of our lives, as
  we become more inescapably aware of bits and pieces of other

people's problems and cultures penetrating our own little worlds, coupled with the sense that everything is moving ever faster, everything is mobile. All this, again, creates excitement but also tension and a sense of bewilderment, as if everything is coming apart, is depthless.

All these and other aspects of globalization are real but they are also intrinsically vague, hard to articulate: they offer 'soft' experiences, which are rather insubstantial, transient and fluctuating. As such, they are hard to explain even to students and therefore it is not surprising that most 'ordinary' people remain rather uninterested in hearing about them and are normally unlikely to take them on board as explanations for their predicament, or for the uncertainties and difficulties coursing through their own lives.

The relative paucity or absence of globality

I, and other global thinkers, misunderstood a central reality relating to globalization. A global consciousness is not the same as the globalization processes that forge and extend the structural economic, trade, institutional and communicative linkages between societies – the scaffolding of a global order that penetrates everyone's life. Moreover, the acceleration and intensification of the processes and connectivities involved in the latter do not necessarily penetrate the subjectivities of individual social actors, though this may happen. Globality refers to a subjective phenomenon whereby individuals build a picture of and form a sense of empathy or emotional solidarity with faraway people they do not know, so to some degree they identify with the needs of all humanity and the planet.

Thus, globalization can and does penetrate and transform the lives of most people in many ways, but this does not mean that social actors understand or recognize such changes for what they are. They may be indifferent to them or in denial about them, preferring instead to fall back on familiar, established local explanations for their experiences of job loss, higher prices, falling wages, deteriorating work conditions, housing shortages, or loss of identity when surrounded by neighbours whose languages, customs and lifestyles are different from their own. Here, the most likely result is that the locals project the blame for their discontentment, anxiety and sense of loss onto (a) the immigrants living in their immediate vicinity and (b) local politicians, perhaps demanding a return to nativism in culture and politics. Why are we not first in line when it comes to handing out resources? Alternatively, they may recognize the role of globalization in their own personal misfortunes, yet demand that their political leaders secede from regional or international organizations and political agreements. They thus retreat behind what Castells calls 'trenches of resistance' instead of urging their governments to seek deeper and more meaningful collaboration with other governments, especially when dealing with problems that are best resolved through joint collaborative policies.

Over-coding the global

I would argue that for some time and still to some extent, a number of global thinkers – I include myself in this category, but not Robin – fundamentally misunderstood what globalization actually is and how it is constituted. In particular, the phenomenon we like to call globalization is, in reality, made up of several overlapping and parallel objective transformations that underpin and reinforce each other but that have different origins and trajectories. Briefly, among these are:

- the industrial rise of Japan in the 1960s, 1970s and 1980s and the Japanization of many Western economies;
- the end of the Cold War and opening up of the East, including the huge increase in the labour force available to capital, plus China's entry into the world economy;
- the rise of formerly 'Third World' industrial nations (such as South Korea and Taiwan) and, more recently, the huge competitive impact of BRIC and other countries on the advanced economies because of their sheer technological competence helped by massive investment in science and higher education;
- a cluster of long-term technological advances in transport – containerization, air freight, huge investments in rail and road across much of the global South – as well as in oil, steel manufacturing and above all IT, with all the possibilities this has created for cheap, instant mass communication;
- the financialization of capital – empowered by digitalization – and the global linkages it has generated as well as its propensity to generate speculative bubbles and predatory capitalism because it rarely engages in the long-term productive investment that creates 'real' wealth and jobs; and
- the rise and predominance of neoliberal ideology, which the USA has been pushing since the late 1970s through the Washington Consensus, exposed most economies to market forces, competition and privatization and this has helped generate work insecurity and the decline of labour power more or less everywhere.

All this has led to:

- a much more competitive, insecure work situation for work forces;

- a fundamental shift in the balance of world military, economic and cultural power, even though for the time being America remains mostly dominant; and
- a huge increase in the pressure on (therefore prices of) and scramble for global resources – food, water, debt finance, minerals, urban spaces and cultivatable land. The collapsing oil price in late 2015 is the exception to this tendency.

My point, however, is that globalization theorists have tended to hijack these transformations and conflate them with something they call 'globalization'. Consequently, they often fail to explain that each of these has its own causal origins and each continues to exercise its own separate logic, dynamics and autonomy in relation to globalization.

This, in turn, has generated an overblown notion of the power and influence that globalization can evoke and exercise, and the direct influence it has over the motivations and orientations of individual social actors. Of course, if we try to establish what the main threads of globalization are, we immediately confront the reality that each exercises its own impact and is in some sense partially independent of the others. In other words, some theorists have tended to endow this thing called globalization with a degree of autonomy and pulling power with respect to other transformations, which in most instances it does not possess. I like to think that Robin and I did not fall into this trap. We always saw that we needed to understand, explain and describe globalization alongside (and in association with) a number of additional transformations. These include Fordism, the impact of the Great Depression and two world wars, the legacy of imperialism, the rise of feminism, the Cold War and Japanization. We also recognized that we needed carefully to delineate those areas in which globalization did influence human behaviour and experience in its own right. Then, I would say that wouldn't I?

It is worth noting that, as Albrow argued, globalization is a condition not a project – though it could become one if governments acted to coordinate their policies more decisively than has so far been evident. Thus, whereas modernity – led by modernizing national elites – expressed the clear purpose of advancing the economic and political influence of the nation in an international order consisting of competing nation-states through a prolonged and multi-faceted project, globalization and the multiple and partly independent processes bound up in it has not been a project in this same sense. Individual nations past and present have entertained ambitions to attain some kind of world domination, but that is not the same as globalization – the mostly accidental, fortuitous, piecemeal, multi-faceted and incomplete unification of the many different cultures and peoples of the world around increasingly shared institutions and joint actions to solve common problems and pursue mutual understanding and respect.

The rejection of globalization – deglobalization – nevertheless demonstrates its centrality if only in a negative sense. Despite having just expressed the need for a more modest and measured account of what globalization is, and its relatively limited influence on shaping the events and changes taking place in the world, I now go on to suggest that the changes associated with it are evident everywhere. Examples include:

- financial integration and the financial crisis;
- the power of global corporations;
- the rise of a now multinational global economic elite;

127

- mass migrations;
- transnational crime;
- tourist flows;
- the gigantic world sporting events that billions watch; and
- the influence of social media, which empower terrorist murderers and international paedophiles, ease family communications and help to construct teenage identities.

What is equally obvious, I would argue, is the presence of globalization in another sense, namely a series of growing reactions to and against it, occurring pretty well everywhere in the world. These reactions have the potential to bring violence, reinforce prejudice and conflict, and drive minorities and sometimes majorities to demand separation. They create political and cultural fragmentation and they often revive ethnic or national identities and affiliations that many assumed had long subsided. In short, several decades of accelerating globalization, in parallel with other changes, have provoked the current era of what we might term angry deglobalization, which consists of serious attempts to move politics in the opposite direction – attempts to reject and even to withdraw from its impact on local lives. Yet, even this deglobalization is tantamount to a kind of globalization.

Of course, the economic crisis of 2008/9 and its continuing aftermath intensified much of this rejection, but I think there is more going on here than merely the reaction to economic insecurities intensified by financial collapse. Thus, falling real incomes, underemployment, job insecurity and the rise of part-time, casual labour associated with outsourcing on a vast scale as well as deindustrialization – what Standing[1] calls the rise of the 'precariat' – and the attack on middle-class incomes and certainties long preceded 2008 and are standard across the advanced economies. But additional changes accompany all this – an ageing population and rising health care costs, relentless technological change that deskills or undermines the work possibilities of many, and the continuing pressure from incoming migrant flows as political turmoil, civil war, poverty, landlessness and much else besides propels ever more destitute and oppressed people to seek refuge in the rich countries.

Indeed, one or both of two things has been occurring. First, there has been a revival and flourishing of atavistic affiliations, demands and protests (often triggering political protest and sometimes violence, or with a potential for violence). Second, since 2001 there have been a number of reactions or responses specifically to globalization that express rejection and hostility to globalization processes, including the demand for political change, which involves some kind of secession or separation from a pre-existing and established political system. Often the two – revival and rejection – are closely linked. Here are a few examples of the strife linked one way or another to the stresses and tensions of globalization, which seem rife all around us.

- the rise of mostly right-wing nationalist parties across Europe (roughly one-third of the votes at the May 2015 election) that are anti-immigrant, nativist, hostile to the EU and, like our own UKIP, calling for our exit from it. Secessionist demands and hostility to large political entities are

---

1. Guy Standing, *The precariat: the new dangerous class* (London: Bloomsbury, 2011).

not confined to minority parties as we can see from the divisions in the Tory Party over Britain's supposed loss of sovereignty in relation to Europe;

- nearer to home, the recent Scottish referendum when nearly half the voters were demanding Scottish secession – in large part because they resent the electoral and economic domination of London and the southeast but also for genuine reasons of national identity;
- the divisions in the Ukraine and Putin's willingness to exploit ethnic Russian identities in the eastern part of the country – and possibly elsewhere in the former USSR where ethnic Russian minorities can be persuaded to believe they are being marginalized; and
- the chaos across North Africa and the Middle East. This is even more horrifying and worrying because it followed the brief period of the 'Arab Spring'. We allowed ourselves to hope that a new era of accountable, secular, democratic government was emerging in which sectarian discrimination, violence, government corruption and the mass suppression of civil rights by security forces or religious extremism might be ending. A century of misguided and exploitative interference in Middle Eastern politics is, of course, partly and perhaps mostly responsible for the ethnic and sectarian splintering and violence evident now. However, deep, unresolved religious, tribal and interregional schisms, coupled with the still vibrant and powerful indigenous economic and political inequalities lying beneath the structures, political boundaries, modern technologies and economic practices that the West had imposed are very evident too.

To all this we could add, among other things,

- the continuing distrust between India and Pakistan;
- China's quarrels with its neighbours, including Japan, over territorial claims;
- the several bloody civil wars that still blight Africa;
- the corrupt regimes that foreign states and businesses bolster;
- Australian anti-immigration sentiments;
- the rigidity of US politics with many in the Republican Party resonantly hostile to any reforms that might hurt the business lobby or reduce inequality even to the point of bringing down the government and the economy; and
- the Tea Party's contempt for federal government and taxation and its apparent desire to return to an earlier nineteenth-century past.

Now, I personally see no immediate prospect of this often-violent reaction against and resistance to globalizing processes leading to many happier and less dangerous changes. Partly, this is because of the inherent complexity of globalization and its related transformations, but also because there is not one change going on here, but, as previously suggested, several things happening simultaneously.

As Robertson famously suggested, globalization means that all the balls are up in the air and anything can happen as we do not know where they might fall. Perhaps, what we need most are new and alternative forms of thinking and protest across many countries driven by a shared project and counter-ideology of global cooperation and the possibility of a less environ-mentally dangerous and more egalitarian form of modernity. Will the next generation be able to produce this?

We have seen Hong Kong students protesting in 2014. We have also seen the worldwide Occupy and Uncut protests earlier. By contrast, we also find second or third generation migrant youths from across Europe rushing out to Syria and Iraq – many originally to fight for democratic political changes but others to re-establish a narrowly sectarian and vicious state hostile to everyone except particular kinds of Sunnis. The recent Jihadists joining ISIS must surely know that they will be involved in murdering civilians.

Of course, it is entirely possible that the note of extreme caution, even pessimism, on which this piece ends reflects my own personal perceptions and state of mind rather more than it picks up on a sense of the real directions in which the world is currently headed. The reader must decide. Certainly, I suspect that Robin might wish to make a much more positive case than I have here.

12. Cosmopolitanism and its Discontents: A Tribute to Robin Cohen

Robert Fine

Robin and I collaborated on a jointly authored chapter in a book he, Robin, co-edited with Steve Vertovec, somewhat ambiguously called *Conceiving Cosmopolitanism*. This collaboration was for me a good experience and built on several years of co-teaching (along with the late and much lamented Peter Gutkind) a course on comparative labour studies that had a strong Third World flavour. The article we co-authored should have been called 'Four cosmopolitan moments' but was actually published as 'Four cosmopolitanism moments', which is awfully close to Gobblygook. Partly on the basis of this chapter, Routledge asked Robin to write a book on cosmopolitanism. He in turn asked me if I would be willing to co-author this book and I agreed. As the result of a characteristically deft Robinesque move, I found myself writing this book as a single author while he pursued his diaspora studies.

To prepare for this event I asked myself what I think the nub of Robin's 'take' on cosmopolitanism is. I do not know if he

Robert Fine

would agree, but I would say that it is in part to challenge the prejudice that cosmopolitanism is the ideology of the elite. In certain Marxist, left-wing and Third World circles, the term 'cosmopolitan' has been largely pejorative. The best-known example is perhaps that of the 'rootless cosmopolitan Jew', an anti-Semitic insult especially favoured by Stalinists after 1945, one that paved the way for all manner of trials and tribulations Jews endured in Eastern Europe in the postwar and cold war period. The phrase 'rootless cosmopolitan Jew' had connotations of disloyalty, lack of patriotism, foreignness and not least worldwide Jewish conspiracy. It was first cousin, as it were, to cognate terms like 'enemy of the people' or indeed 'enemy of the human species'. Here cosmopolitanism was identified with what we might call a 'bad universalism'.

Robin (together with Steve, myself and others) has pointed out that such pejorative uses of the term 'cosmopolitanism' still endure today within sociology and indeed progressive social thinking more generally. Critics of cosmopolitanism have lined up to characterize it as the 'class consciousness of frequent travellers' (in the now famous words of Craig Calhoun), of corporate managers and intergovernmental bureaucrats, tax dodgers and jet-setting academics – anyone with 'expensive tastes and a globetrotting lifestyle' as Bruce Robbins put it. The noble term 'world citizen' is decried from this perspective as the idealized expression of those who renounce the normal obligations of national citizenship – namely paying one's share of taxes and contributing to democratic life. Before we can say Amazon or Starbucks, the cosmopolitan is turned into the 'cosmocrat' who runs the City and gets up the noses of all right-thinking people, and then into the 'cosmoprat' who floats ethereally above the world and prides himself on his superiority.

Well, the great strength not just of Robin's work but also of his whole attitude to life is to redirect our focus towards the cosmopolitanism of non-elites, of the have-nots and, especially, of migrants and refugees. He is interested in what is sometimes called 'everyday' or 'actually existing' cosmopolitanism. This is where ordinary people create hybrid cultures based on a pastiche of local, national and global motifs and styles. It is where the experience of travel on open rickety boats has nothing in common with the frequent flyer, where home can no longer be where one comes from (a place where there may be no chance of returning) but only where one is going to (often an imaginary and elusive destination). Or, perhaps it is where one currently is (since the so-called 'transit migrant' has become the figurative symbol of our age). Robin's interest is in the extraordinary cosmopolitan competences required by ordinary people to live with the contradictions they experience in the modern age – to handle multiple affiliations, to mediate plural loyalties, to encounter other cultures, to validate the complexity of relationships, not least to deal with the 'global risks' that are involved in these very difficult and demanding social relations.

It is no accident that, in our joint chapter, one of the 'four cosmopolitanism moments' that Robin wrote about was the 'Zeno moment' in ancient Athens. Here, he argued that the idea of cosmopolitanism was the brainchild of radicals who confronted and resisted the narrow notions of citizenship attached to the city-state. Cosmopolitanism was conceived by philosophers like the 'cynic' Diogenes and the stoic Zeno, who believed there could be no rightful laws, no commanding temples, no valid sense of Greek superiority over barbarians, and, indeed, no legitimate city-state. Cosmopolitan ideas went down like a bacon sandwich at a Barmitvah. The fact that Zeno was a foreigner, a 'metic' from Cyprus, and usually called a 'Semite', did not endear him – or the universal humanism he espoused – to the authorities. For Robin, this was the proof that cosmopolitanism was originally the conviction of the marginalized and the powerless and that it is onto this legacy that we need to hold today.

So, for me, one of the great strengths of Robin's work is to challenge the claim that cosmopolitanism can be reduced to an ideology of the privileged classes in revolt against the restraints imposed by nation-states. He also challenges the somewhat contradictory claim that Zeno and his spiritual descendants (like Kant in particular) are simply abstract thinkers, remote from reality, wishfully imagining they can live in accordance with general principles and, as Michael Ignatieff put it, misguidedly abandoning all 'natural ties'. How right Robin is to question this kind of charge. We hear it repeated a thousand times today that the problem with the cosmopolitans is that they have no roots in the nation, no divisions to show, no boots on the ground, and that they are the losers of history. Sometimes, cosmopolitan solidarity requires something other than a calculus concerning who will be victorious and who defeated.

Similarly, Robin and I wrote about Kant, the great cosmopolitan philosopher of the late eighteenth century. He may have had his racial and colonial prejudices; he may never have seen the world or left Konigsberg; he may have framed his philosophy in terms of abstract principles. However, he not only learned the art of self-criticism (his political philosophy became ever more radical with age), but he also learned to challenge the injustices of the whole European state system. He challenged its faith in absolute sovereignty, its unregulated interstate wars, its charade of international law, and its phoney justifications of colonialism in terms of the rights of colonizers. True, Kant's cosmopolitanism fought against the tide of nationalism that followed the French Revolution, but should this be conceived as its weakness?

I do not know what Robin will think of this but I have recently been reading the essays and literature of Stefan Zweig, the great Austrian Jewish writer of the interwar period. Zweig has often been accused of whistling a cosmopolitan tune while Europe burnt. Well, he was certainly from the Austrian Jewish elite and a highly successful author to boot. But his cosmopolitanism was no whistling matter in the 1930s. His revolt against nationalism, his disgust with militarism, his belief in the creation of a European Union, his commitment to international law, his recognition of the unity of the human race, his understanding of differences (including Jewishness) as an essential part of what we mean by common humanity – all this cosmopolitanism came at a human cost. It is the human quality of cosmopolitanism that I think Robin has been able to touch and to feel.

13. Global Perspectives

Barbara Harriss-White

 In 1997 when I proposed a Wolfson public lecture series (a series my college organizes annually) on the subject of globalization and insecurity, a senior fellow quashed the idea saying that globalization 'wasn't received English'.

Nevertheless, in 1999 Wolfson did mount a multidisciplinary series. Each speaker was asked to address two questions – (i) what new forms of insecurity had been generated by globalization and (ii) what was being done about them? Distinguished speakers focused on different aspects – for example Valpy Fitzgerald on finance, John Kay on business, Sue Willetts on weapons, Ian Brownlie on international law, David Held and Samit Amin on politics, Wolfgang Sachs on environment and so on. It was fairly terrifying to sit through.

Robin gave the lecture on labour and that is how we met – formerly I had known him by reputation. He gave an excellent talk, surprisingly upbeat, about labour not as a narrow sectional interest, but as the general representatives of humanity. He argued that the obituaries for trade unions were premature, giving many examples of trade union activism from developing countries. He wound up by saying that, while the revolutionary potential of the labour movement might have dissipated, organized labour was in the vanguard of the political advance of 'social justice, public services and democratic rights'.

The book of the lectures – *Globalization and insecurity* – is out there on Amazon. Published just before or after 9/11, it sank without trace – since 'security' was so rapidly redefined and narrowed in the War on Terror. I feel responsible for Robin's only publishing failure.

Anyway, this session's two speakers, Paul Kennedy and Robert Fine, have not been guilty of such a crime, having collaborated and published very successfully with Robin on globalization and cosmopolitanism respectively.

Coming out of the presentations and discussions were some interesting points – at least ones I remember:

- how social science theorizes contradictory processes;
- intellectual competences needed to understand globalization;
- how globalization is defined through connectivity but also involves scale, new social configurations, institutions and powers, flows and the impact on nature;
- misattribution of complex social changes to 'globalization';
- ordinary global citizens and their understanding of cause and effect (human nature, politicians and the Chinese!) and subaltern cosmopolitanism;
- the many tensions of cosmopolitanism;
- obstacles to globalization and why they were so hard to foresee; and
- how most of the world's people now depend on a fantastically complex division of labour combined with expert systems,

which Martin Rees's new institute at Cambridge regards as exceedingly vulnerable to small ('extremist') events.

We could have spent more time on the underbelly of globalization and its articulation to the formal and 'organized' play of finance, trade, political power and the movement of different classes of people.

Praise to Paul and Robert for fine case studies of academics as activists and for the academic life and one of activism – and to the organizers for their inspired choices of eras, institutions, themes, ideas and substance as Robin and others saw it, along with Robin's work as seen by others. It takes a giant in the field for this richness to be possible.

14. The Flight to Work: A Review of Robin Cohen's *The New Helots*[1]

Jeff Crisp

A great deal of the existing literature on refugees either explicitly or implicitly draws a clear distinction between those people who leave their own country involuntarily, because their life or liberty are in danger ('refugees' and 'asylum seekers'), and those who voluntarily move in response to generalized hardship and the desire to improve their material circumstances ('migrants'). Given the provenance of the literature, this is not surprising. For refugee rights groups and pro-asylum activists, it is essential to retain a legal distinction between the two groups, lest the claims of the former are weakened. For the Office of the UN High Commissioner for Refugees the distinction is necessary to prevent an unmanageable extension of the organization's mandate. For scholars in the emerging field of 'refugee studies', it is convenient to work within a discrete conceptual framework. While some efforts have recently been made to study refugees in

---

1. First published in *Journal of Refugee Studies*, vol. 1, no. 1, 1988, pp. 85–7.

tandem with other groups of 'involuntary migrants',[2] these have focused on officially organized movements (forcible relocation programmes and expulsions) rather than apparently 'spontaneous' cross border migrations.

In his wonderfully stimulating and synoptic new book, *The New Helots*,[3] Robin Cohen acknowledges that economic migrations, 'the flight to work' as he calls it, are, in a causal sense, 'largely distinct from the movements of political refugees or those caught up in the misfortunes of war'. But at the same time, his analysis of 'migrants in the international division of labour' raises with a rare degree of clarity the conceptual problem of distinguishing 'voluntary' and 'involuntary' population movements.

Drawing on an extraordinarily wide range of empirical and theoretical literature, and on his own research in southern and West Africa, the Caribbean, Hong Kong, St Helena and the United Kingdom, Cohen argues, contrary to Marx, that a major engine of capitalism has been its ability to exploit successive cohorts of 'unfree', 'semi-free', or 'quasi-free' labour. These include African slaves in the New World, indentured Indians in Asia and the Caribbean, and conscripted labour in colonial Africa.

Contrary to Wallerstein, he argues that the use of unfree labour is not confined to the 'periphery' of international capitalism, but can also be found at its 'core' – children and Irish migrants in nineteenth-century Britain, camp labour in the Soviet Union and slave labour in Nazi Germany. Continuing his critique of Wallerstein, Cohen argues that the contemporary

---

2. See *Refugees: dynamics of displacement, independent commission on international humanitarian issues* (London: Zed Books, 1986).
3. Robin Cohen, *The new helots: migrants in the international division of labour* (Aldershot: Avebury/Gower Publishing Group, 1987).

deployment of unfree labour takes place not within the context of a 'world system' but within 'regional political economies'. These are economies in which the dominant state or states play 'a central and directing role in the structuring of a division of labour, in the legitimation of an involuntary labour regime ... the recruitment and regulation of coerced workers ... and policing of the frontiers of the metropolitan area'. The theme of political control provides an important reason for seeing the bulk of modern (post-1945) international migrants as involuntary labourers. They are, says Cohen, 'generally distinguished by their exclusion from or restricted opportunities to acquire the full rights of citizenship in core countries'.

In the central chapters of the book, Cohen develops this thesis with respect to three different regional political economies. At the same time, he uses these case studies to examine three contemporary theoretical issues – general theories of migration in relation to the USA and its circum-Caribbean labour reserves; the 'reproduction of labour power' debate in relation to southern Africa; and the so-called 'structural necessity of migration' issue in relation to western Europe.

In the last of these succinct but persuasive discussions, Cohen concludes that both orthodox and radical economists have exaggerated the extent to which migrant labour was a permanent solution for European capital. As many potential migrants and asylum seekers have discovered, they are no longer needed by capital or welcomed by the state: the 'structural requirements' of business are now best met outside the national economy, through the export of capital to low-wage areas in other parts of the world.

This observation also points to Cohen's next area of concern, namely the way in which capital and state seek to control the flow of unfree labour through 'regulatory apparatuses directed against free worker mobility'. These include immigration checks, inter-state labour contracts and 'influx control' in Southern Africa; the guestworker system, assisted repatriation (and, Cohen might have added, restrictive asylum legislation) in West Germany; and legislative controls and physical interventions in the USA, where refugee policy has become inextricably linked with general immigration policy. As Cohen accurately observes, 'the immediate political crisis surrounding the admission of Cubans and Haitian refugees ... served to 'dramatise the general incapacity of the US state to translate its ideological utterances and elaborate regulatory apparatuses into effective administrative practice'.

But, Cohen forcibly reminds us, people who have in a very real sense been 'compelled' if not 'forced' to migrate and sell their labour power are not passive victims of the structures that constrain their life opportunities. Even extraordinarily powerful and authoritarian states have found it impossible to transform the 'new helots' into pliant tools of industrial and economic management. 'Illegal' workers constantly evade the traps set for them and engage in both 'open' and 'hidden' forms of resistance to their subordination. Indeed, as Cohen indicates in his final chapter, a critique of the 'new international division of labour' theory, the success of such resistance has itself been one of the factors prompting the export of capital to the newly industrializing countries of Southeast Asia, where a new cohort of unfree labour can be exploited. In the author's depressing words, the newest of the new helots constitute 'a labour force that presents few of the demands for social and industrial rights that even the South African government and companies are slowly having to recognize'.

This book is a formidable piece of comparative sociology and history. For this reviewer, its main interest was to be found less in its provocative central thesis than in its ability to trace the connections between a wide range of apparently diverse contemporary events. Despite the fluency of Cohen's style and his gift for the telling phrase, it is by no means an easy work and, to be properly comprehended, demands an acquaintance with a very substantial body of theoretical and empirical literature. But anyone who is working in the area of 'involuntary migration' should read it, read it again, and then ask why the existing literature on refugees has been so poorly informed or influenced by the analytical tools of radical political economy.

15. Tar Baby: Migration and Culture

Gunvor Jónsson

This presentation is going to be about migration and culture. I am busy reading Toni Morrison's book *Tar Baby*. The tar baby refers to a 'sticky topic' that grabs hold of you, metaphorically speaking, and the more you try to fight it, the more entangled you get. I guess the culture concept is a bit like a tar baby. As Robin and I wrote in a joint publication, 'precise definitions of this difficult, multifaceted and capacious word somehow seem to elude us. The idea of culture is so tantalizingly out of reach, yet so necessary for us to grasp.'[1]

I first met Robin when I started working at the International Migration Institute (IMI), while Stephen Castles was still the director. Robin used to come around IMI and we would have little chats. When Robin learnt that I had done my master's degree in anthropology, he commented that it seemed that anthropologists still had not really worked out what to do with

---

1. Toni Morrison, *Tar baby* (New York: Alfred A. Knopf, 1981); R. Cohen and G. Jónsson, 'Connecting culture and migration', in R. Cohen and G. Jónsson (eds) *Migration and culture* (Cheltenham: Edward Elgar, 2011, p. xi).

'culture' and that they appeared to have kind of given up on the concept (or something along those lines).

To some extent, I was probably one of those anthropologists to whom Robin was referring. When I studied for my BA in South Africa, I learnt how Afrikaner anthropologists had theoretically conceptualized a notion of culture to justify apartheid intellectually. Then, on returning to Denmark for my master's degree, I was struck by the xenophobic rhetoric of Danish right-wing nationalists and the very essentialist understandings of Danish identity, which seemed to echo those apartheid notions of culture. These experiences made me rather wary of culture, and quite prone to deconstruct the concept.

However, I think working with Robin made me re-engage with the culture concept in a much more constructive way. When Robin became director of IMI, among all the many things he did, he put culture on the migration research agenda, and he involved me in that effort, for which I am very grateful.

Therefore, this talk is going to be about some of the intersections between culture and migration that Robin has inspired me to think about.

Migration and culture book

One thing that Robin and I did was to edit a volume on culture and migration. Editing the book with Robin was an exciting attempt to carve out the contours of an emerging perspective, if not a field within migration studies, focused on cultural dimensions and drawing on insights developed in, for example, cultural studies, anthropology and sociology. The book brought together literature that was scattered in different and sometimes little known journals and websites, but which clearly spoke to each other. The book really made a point of drawing out the varied and exciting ways in which theories and observations related to culture could be applied to migration research, both in terms of studying the processes, as well as the outcomes of migration – to put it simplistically, the book considered both the migration of culture and the culture of migration.

I think that a positivist approach, seeking objective facts and truths, informs a lot of the established research into migration processes. But the book I edited with Robin illustrated that it is certainly also possible meaningfully to examine migration processes by using a more critical approach that accounts for subjectivity, meaning, power, conflict and resistance. Something I am very interested in is the socio-cultural dimensions of migration processes – particularly the ideas, values and norms that regulate and facilitate migratory behaviour and make the endeavour of migration meaningful.[2] The introduction that Robin and I wrote for the book gave me the opportunity to develop some of my thoughts about the 'culture of migration' concept, drawing on research I conducted on

---

2. R. Cohen and G. Jónsson, 'Connecting culture and migration', in R. Cohen and G. Jónsson (eds) *Migration and culture* (Cheltenham: Edward Elgar, 2011); G. Jónsson, *The mirage of migration: migration aspirations and immobility in a Malian Soninke village* (Institute for Anthropology, University of Copenhagen, Denmark, 2007); G. Jónsson, 'Imagination and connectedness: consumption of global forms in a Malian village', paper presented to European Conference on African Studies (Uppsala, Sweden, 2011); G. Jónsson, 'Non-migrant, sedentary, immobile, or "left behind"? Reflections on the absence of migration', *IMI Working Paper Series*, no. 39 (International Migration Institute, University of Oxford, 2011); G. Jónsson, 'Migration, identity and immobility in a Malian Soninke village', in S. G. K. Schielke (ed.) *The global horizon: expectations of migration in Africa and beyond* (Leuven: Leuven University Press, 2012).

young men in Mali in West Africa. Since our book project, I have used some of those thoughts about migration and culture for my doctoral thesis, which is an anthropological study, based on fieldwork in the Senegalese capital Dakar in West Africa, where I looked at the migration and mobilities of female traders from the neighbouring country, Mali.

So, what I shall do now is first briefly discuss some of the research on the cultural dimensions of migration processes. Then afterwards I will present an aspect of my current doctoral research that looks specifically at the meanings of mobility and migration among Malian women in Senegal.

Cultural dimensions of migration processes

Scholars have applied the concept of 'cultures of migration'[3] to analyse normative and socio-cultural aspects of migration processes.[4] In mainstream migration research, this concept is used to describe 'a continuous commitment to migration that

---

3. M. de Bruijn, H. van Dijk and R. van Dijk, 'Cultures of travel: Fulbe pastoralists in central Mali and Pentecostalism in Ghana', in M. de Bruijn, R. van Dijk and D. Foeken (eds), *Mobile Africa: changing patterns of movement in Africa and beyond* (Leiden: Brill, 2001) refer to 'cultures of travel' and 'mobile cultures' instead.

4. See L. Åkesson, *Making a life: meanings of migration in Cape Verde* (Ph.D. thesis, Göteborg University, 2004); S. Ali, '"Go West young man": the culture of migration among Muslims in Hyderabad, India', *Journal of Ethnic and Migration Studies* (vol. 33, pp. 37–58); J. H. Cohen, *The culture of migration in southern Mexico* (Austin: University of Texas Press, 2004); J. H. Cohen and I. Sirkeci, *Cultures of migration: the global nature of contemporary mobility* (Austin: University of Texas Press, 2011); Cohen and Jónsson, op. cit., 2011; de Bruijn et al., op. cit., 2001; H. P. Hahn and G. Klute (eds) *Cultures of migration: African perspectives* (Münster: Lit Verlat, 2007); Jónsson, op. cit., 2007; W. Kandel and D. Massey, 'The culture of Mexican migration: a theoretical and empirical analysis', *Social Forces* (vol. 80, 2002, pp. 981–1004).

becomes embedded in society and evolves into a set of distinctive socio-cultural processes, usually in contexts where migration patterns from particular areas of origin to particular destinations are regular, continuous, and occurring on a large scale'.[5] Such processes are not confined to migrants; non-migrants observe migrants to whom they are socially connected and seek to emulate their migratory behaviour, while migration becomes so deeply rooted that young people expect to live and work abroad.[6]

In fact, most people attach certain meanings and values to migration, and all processes of migration to some extent reflect socially acquired knowledge and behaviour. Hence, one might argue that *all* migrants have some form of 'culture of migration'.[7] I have to admit that I find the term 'culture of migration' somewhat problematic. Similar to the notion of 'a culture of poverty', there is a risk of conceiving of culture as this dominant and subjugating force that people cannot escape and that leads to entirely homogenous ways of thinking and acting. I think it helps if we introduce concepts like discourse and power, or hegemony, as well as meanings and imaginaries.[8] This allows us to examine different coexisting understandings and perceptions of migration, as well as conflicts over and resistance to dominant discourses on migration. It also inspires a more nuanced exploration of the different meanings of migration, not just in different parts of the world, but also according to for example

---

5. Cohen and Jónsson, op. cit., 2011, p. xxiv.
6. Ibid.; Kandel and Massey, op. cit., 2002.
7. Cohen and Jónsson, op. cit., 2011.
8. Cf. H. P. Hahn and G. Klute (eds) *Cultures of migration: African perspectives* (Münster: Lit Verlag, 2007); and S. Schielke and K. Graw (eds) *The global horizon* (Belgium: Leuven University Press, 2012).

age, gender, class, or ethnicity. Let me now turn to my doctoral research to show how I have used these ideas to examine the meanings of migration as they pertain to Malian women in Senegal, West Africa.

Femininity, mobility and migration

Scholars working on West Africa have pointed out that social groups often have their own norms and ideologies to define desirable and undesirable migration, which render some forms of migration normative and others socially illegitimate.[9] Several recent studies have examined the meanings, imaginaries and cultures of migration in relation to Malians and other West African people.[10] Meanwhile, such studies tend to focus

---

9. S. Findley, 'Social appearances and economic realities of female migration in rural Mali', in *United Nations expert group meeting on feminization of internal migration, Aguascalientes (Mexico), 22–25 October 1991* (New York: United Nations, 1993); C. Z. Guilmoto, 'Institutions and migrations: short-term versus long-term moves in rural West Africa', *Population Studies*, vol. 52, 1998, pp. 85–103; M. Lambert, 'Politics, patriarchy, and new traditions', in H. P. Hahn and G. Klute (eds) *Cultures of migration* (Berlin: Lit Verlag, 2007); H. Olofson, 'The Hausa wanderer and structural outsiderhood: an emic and etic analysis', in R. Mansel Prothero and M. Chapman (eds) *Circulation in third world countries* (London: Routledge and Kegan Paul, 1985).
10. For example, S. Bredeloup, 'L'aventurier: une figure de la migration africaine', *Cahiers internationaux de Sociologie*, vol. 125, pp. 281–306; P. Gaibazzi, 'Migration, Soninke young men and the dynamics of staying behind: the Gambia' (Ph.D. dissertation, Università degli Studi di Milano-Bicocca, 2010); Hahn and Klute, 'Introduction', op. cit., 2007; Jónsson, op. cit., 2012; Schielke and Graw, op. cit., 2012; M. Timera, 'Les migrations des jeunes Sahéliens: affirmation de soi et emancipation', *Autrepart*, vol. 18, 2001, pp. 37–49; B. Whitehouse, *Migrants and strangers in an African city: exile, dignity, belonging* (Bloomington: Indiana University Press, 2012).

on men and a similar analytical approach is rarely extended to the women in this region, so that is what I am going to do here.

My fieldwork in Dakar focused on both mobile and settled female traders from Mali, the neighbouring country. Mobile traders are known as *bana-banas* (those who travel back and forth selling or buying goods). I also looked at Malian market traders (who had immigrated to Dakar). Many of these women were heads of their own households; many were single, whether unmarried, divorced or widowed.

I shall now, in an attempt to examine the kinds of behaviours and meanings with which they were associated, look at the various mobilities in which the Malian women engaged. I start with the simple act of walking, then move on to travel and, finally, consider change of residence. While examining these mobilities, I shall also reflect on how they were associated – or not – with 'femininity'.

Women walking

The following is about an older Malian man called Djiby, who was informally teaching me Bamanankan (which is the language my informants spoke). One day Djiby was teaching me the adverbs 'slowly' and 'fast' and somehow ended up talking about perceived differences between men and women. According to Djiby:

> Women take their time – they walk slowly to the market, eat slowly and they don't run and do sports. Men are fast; if they take their time, they are like women. Men should push themselves to go faster. If a man is very slow, people compare him to a woman. If you say about a man that he

is like a woman, it means he is slow or lazy. They will say that, 'he cannot follow the rhythm of men.' If you walk with a woman, you have to slow yourself down. But there are some women who are fast, like men. If a woman is fast, you can tell her, 'you are like a man.'

Indeed, many of my female informants had a distinctive slow and graceful pace, an almost sensual way of walking through the streets, aware that they would be looked at. Their slow pace also allowed them to scan the surroundings, so they tended to spot people they knew, and would take the time to stop and greet them. Walking for these women was thus a highly social act and not simply a means of getting from one location to another. Finally, the wrapper that most women wore prevented them from taking long steps; if they walked too fast it would get pulled out of position. The wrapper thus helped to set the 'female pace' (cf. Young 1980: 142 for observations of women walking in Western society).[11]

This all suggested to me that proper feminine behaviour implied controlled bodily comportment and restricted forms of mobility. However, in many ways, the female traders with whom I worked did not conform to this feminine ideal. Many female *bana-banas* seemed to walk in a rather 'masculine' way with distinctively long and fast strides that differed from the graceful, slow pace of other Malian women. I once spent the day purchasing goods in different shops in downtown Dakar with a *bana-bana* whose name was Ramatoullaye. Ramatoullaye went

---

11. See I. M. Young, 'Throwing like a girl: a phenomenology of feminine body comportment motility and spatiality' (*Human Studies*, vol. 3, 1980, pp. 137–56) p. 142 for observations of women walking in Western society.

in front, with me and her two young male apprentices following in lockstep. She walked determinedly with long, fast strides. This was on a Friday during the Ramadan (my informants were Muslim), and the two men were fasting, while Ramatoullaye permitted herself a very modest lunch and some water to drink. By afternoon, the men were starved, but Ramatoullaye kept pushing them to continue, while they kept lagging behind and complaining that they were tired. She moaned when the men stopped to pray at 2.00 p.m. because there was no time for a break, she insisted. At one point, Ramatoullaye even walked straight past her own local hosts, as she was too fast to notice them. Observing this, it appeared as if the very fixed gender roles that Djiby had told me about were reversed or perhaps out of force.

Women's journeys

My informant Nana, who was a *bana-bana* from Bamako, often had arguments with her husband because he was unhappy about her staying in Dakar for long periods. Once we were out shopping and, as we were strolling, I asked her if she had bought anything for her husband, as it was customary for *bana-banas* to bring back little gifts after their journey to Dakar. 'This time I haven't,' she replied:

> I am angry with him. He doesn't like that I travel. When I leave, he asks me when I am going to return; when I return, he tells me I spent a long time away. Is that any good? I am busy working. But they think that if you travel and you spend a long time away, that you are up to something. That you are going to cheat on them. But me, I am busy working! Ah!

154

Nana was in fact the main breadwinner of her small household, which included an under-employed husband and Nana's teenage daughter from a previous relationship.

The association of female travel with promiscuous sexual behaviour is a longstanding one. The early literature on female migration in West Africa created a stereotypical image of female migrants as actual or potential prostitutes.[12] These days female migrants' sexuality still attracts great attention, for example in relation to trafficking or HIV/AIDS. However, I think that concerns about mobile women's promiscuity or sexual vulnerability sometimes mask a deeper concern about women's autonomous migration posing a (potential) threat to the socio-economic structure of patriarchal families and communities. For example, a Malian man told that me he did not want his wife to travel because then she would get to know money and would stop looking after her husband and their home, and their marriage would disintegrate.

However, I also sensed that the norms were changing. For example, *ka yaala* means to stroll or wander, or even to roam about. A woman who goes *yaala* is someone who goes out at night or is always seen in the street, I was told. In my Bamanankan class I was taught that men were reluctant to marry young women who went *yaala*. When I asked a couple of *banabanas* if it was a problem if a woman went *yaala*, they responded that, 'that was in the past or out in the bush that they don't like that. but today, a woman can go anywhere she wants to. If you love her, you marry her; it doesn't matter if she goes *yaala*.'

---

12. R. Pittin, 'Migration of women in Nigeria: the Hausa case', *International Migration Review*, vol. 18, 1984, pp. 1293–314; N. Sudarkasa, 'Women and migration in contemporary West Africa', *Signs*, vol. 3, 1977, pp. 178–89.

These women were contesting such a narrow definition of 'femininity' and arguing that the norms were changing.

Change of residence

I noted several interesting parallels between the life-course of Malian women and conceptions and experiences of migration. In this regard, two particularly pertinent concepts were *dunnan* and *tunga* – so I am going to teach you a bit of Bamanakan now, which is the language my Malian informants were speaking! I have already told you about *ka yaala*.

Dunnan broadly means stranger. Upon marriage, a Malian woman moves out of her parental house to join a new household, where her husband and his family live. There is a Bamanankan expression, '*kòyònmuso dunnan don*', which literally means the bride is a stranger. When the bride comes to live with her husband and his relatives, she is not yet integrated into the family. The people in the husband's house would refer to her as *dunnanmuso*, meaning the foreign/ unfamiliar/new woman.

In Bamanankan, the word *tunga* refers to a place that 'is not home' or where you are 'not at home'. Some informants used *tunga* in a broad sense where they refer to it as any place that is not one's natal home; but others insisted on a more narrow definition whereby *tunga* referred to a distant, foreign place or country where one was unfamiliar with the people or surroundings. Hence, the destination of migrants was considered *tunga*.

I asked my female informants whether the house of one's husband could also be considered *tunga*; but they disagreed on this point. Some said it definitely was *tunga* because it was not your home ('*so*' in Bamanan) or where you came from ('*bòyòrò*'). Others said your husband's house was only *tunga* if it was located far away from your home, but not if you lived in the same village or your husband's parents lived just up the road.

Women informants explained that after having moved out, married women came to be considered *dunnan* (strangers) in their parents' home. When they went there to visit they would be referred to as *dunnan*. If a woman got divorced she would often be expected to go and live with her parents and when she returned to her father's house, she would be considered a *dunnan* – a stranger. If a woman's husband died she might be allowed to stay in the house, but frequently less fortunate widows were chased out of their homes upon their husband's death. Hence, not only marriage, but also divorce and widow-hood were often defined by the woman's mobility and an accompanying existential experience of strangerhood, similar to that of migrants.

In Bamanankan there is a saying, '*Tunga tè danbè don*', which means that there is no dignity in *tunga*, or that a person has no value in foreign places. The message is that when you migrate (go to *tunga*), the people there will not know you or your background, and they will not care about it; therefore, in *tunga*, you have to put aside your pride. This resembles the way a new bride is expected to behave in her husband's home, where humility, endurance and tolerance are believed to ease her trans-ition from being a *dunnan* (stranger) to becoming a familiar member of the family.

Another common interpretation of the proverb is that since people do not know you in *tunga* your reputation is not at stake if you do humiliating jobs or live in conditions that you would never accept back home. That the Malian women I met were to various degrees unknown strangers in Dakar allowed them to ignore some of the norms to which they were subjected back in

Mali. For example, many Malian women were trading aphrodisiacs and this occupation was well known to their husbands and friends. However, I was told that if these women were back in Mali they would hide the fact that they were selling such things. My informant Oumou was selling a snack made from a Malian product that earned her very little profit. She explained, 'I cannot tell my mother back in Mali that I am selling this. If my mother knew, she would tell me that this is not work. This thing I am selling, you only sell that to get by. What I am doing now, that is not real work.'

Tunga also provided a certain level of anonymity that allowed the Malian women to reinvent themselves. Indeed, I often heard gossip about Malian women 'on the loose' in Dakar, who had apparently lost all sense of modesty. They were roaming about, defying their husbands' demands, having numerous sexual partners, or spending money that was not theirs.

Conclusion

Examining the meanings of female mobility can provide a window onto what constitutes normative 'feminine' behaviour and what is resistance to or subversion of the norms. I would also argue that, by looking at the ways female mobilities are conceived and perceived, we might get a better understanding of why and how these women migrate – or not – and what sorts of consequences migration might have for the women and the wider socio-cultural contexts between which they move. In this way, an approach that accounts for culture and for the perspectives and experiences, as expressed by the people we study, can enhance understandings of the processes and outcomes of migration. Therefore, I guess, what I am suggesting is, embrace the tar baby of culture and migration!

16. Diaspora Studies: Robin's Impact on Me

Alan Gamlen

In this brief tribute to Robin I hope to acknowledge Robin's impact on me in three ways. First, by changing the world in ways I have found interesting to study; second by helping me and others think through ways of critically reflecting on these changes; and third by being a mentor and role model.

How to measure impact? Let's begin with some data on impact that everyone loves – citation counts. Below I have pasted a screenshot from an online tool developed by Google, called 'Ngram Viewer'. You can type in any word and it searches for it in a corpus of well over five million books comprising 500 billion words. It plots the frequency of the word over time going back to the seventeenth century and in some cases before. This tool is an especially useful tool for gauging the impact of scholars who, by simple misfortune of birth, lived before the age of detailed citation data.

Figure 1: Contrary to the stylized facts, the Beatles were never bigger than Jesus

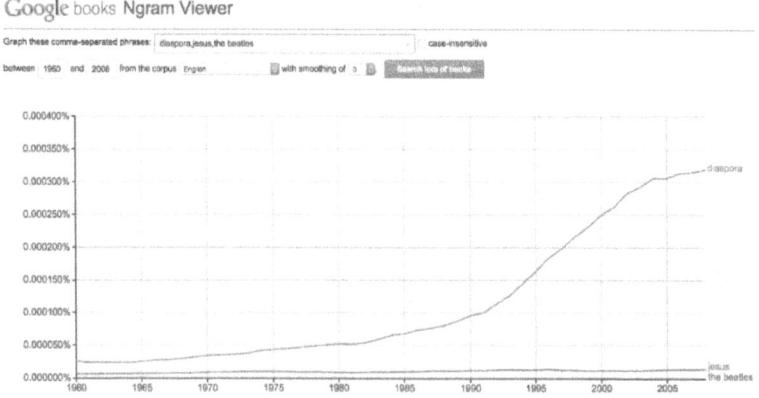

Using this new technology we can put to bed many old controversies that have dogged scholarship during the period of Robin's academic career, beginning in the 1960s. For example, if you look along the x-axis and the first line above it, Figure 1 provides no empirical support for John Lennon's famous assertion that 'the Beatles are bigger than Jesus.' In fact, as the figure shows, since their formation in 1960, the Beatles have never been as highly cited as Jesus. Clearly, that statement should have been peer-reviewed prior to publication (but then again, those were revolutionary times). However, the more important message from Figure 1 lies in the rise of the term diaspora, apparently dwarfing the citation counts of the Beatles and those of Our Saviour, and clearly suggesting a gap in the market for a rock band entitled 'Diaspora'. One fruitful possibility would be 'Robin Cohen and the diasporas' (but this is a matter for future research).[1]

---

1. Health warning: this is not a real piece of research. It is a joke.

Jokes aside, the term diaspora has undoubtedly become a keyword in social science during the course of Robin's career. At the start of this period the word was an esoteric academic term, applied to a few groups that were defined by traumatic dispersion. By the end of that period, however, it had spread far, far beyond academia and made a huge impact on the world of policy and politics. I have heard Robin modestly say that he merely 'caught the wave' of diaspora studies, implying that the timing of his own career and the emergence of diaspora as a key social science concept since the 1960s is merely a coincidence, but there is causation as well as correlation in this pattern. Robin's work has introduced a new comparative dimension to the study of diaspora and has suggested broadening the focus of the term in ways that have defined a field of study ever since.

Now back to the citation counts (sorry for the digression). Robin's work has been cited thousands of times, including by a generation of politicians and officials in origin countries keen to court 'their diasporas'. Recently, two of my graduate students found that around a third of all governments in the world had documented some form of official definition of the word 'diaspora' in order to guide policy towards emigrants and their descendants – many of them citing Robin's work. In this sense, Robin's work on diasporas has changed the way people think and act when organizing world politics.

My research takes off from this starting point, examining these policies, which in some countries are now managed by formal government offices dedicated to the purpose. Well over half of all states now have at least one such diaspora institution. Most are departments or similar units within wider existing ministries, such as the Irish Abroad Unit within the Irish Department of Foreign Affairs. However, an increasing number are fully fledged 'diaspora ministries' such as the Ministry of Overseas Indian Affairs, or Serbia's Ministry for Religion and Diaspora.

Figure 2: Number of states with diaspora institutions, by type, 1936–2014

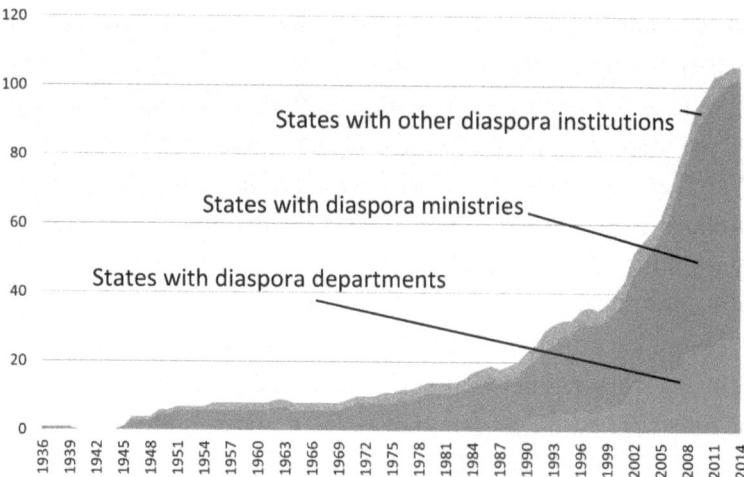

This is not necessarily an unmitigated good thing. These institutions violate some conventional rules of international politics by projecting state authority beyond state borders and claiming the loyalties of people living in foreign territories. They may interfere with both migrants and non-migrants in ways that could be considered illiberal, and they may provide legitimacy to irredentist projects. It should not go unnoticed that the Russian Foreign Ministry justified Russia's recent annexation of the Crimean Peninsula in terms of protecting the interests of Russian people living abroad. 'Diaspora engagement' can clearly have a more sinister side than is sometimes suggested.

Nevertheless, before it sounds like I am blaming Robin for all of this, it is important to recognize that his work has encouraged those of us interested in diaspora politics to reflect critically on these trends. For example, I will always remember how, at the outset of my research in this area, Robin encouraged me to look through 'the state' down into underlying social groups, treating it as a disaggregated entity in a way that is more difficult for scholars in international relations, one field in which the topic of state–diaspora relations has recently taken root. Reading Robin's work on identity and creolization has also helped me and others to think through more normative questions such as whether or not 'engaging diasporas' is a product of ethnic nationalism or of governments with a more cosmopolitan vision. His works have provided many of the schema through which researchers view this area.

Finally, Robin has been a personal mentor in various ways since I first visited his Warnborough Road garret to enthuse about diasporas, but also a mentor to my doctoral supervisors Steven Vertovec and Alisdair Rogers, and a thesis examiner to my previous employer, Ian Goldin. In this godfather-like role, Robin has influenced me in many ways directly and indirectly for more than a decade. I first visited the Gardener's Arms with Robin – the pub in which the Oxford migration crowd has been dining weekly for many years, and which became an incubator for many networks and initiatives. One of these was the journal *Migration Studies*, which I first proposed over a pint to Nick Van Hear in 2007, and which Robin helped mentor into existence several years later. Another was the Oxford Diasporas Programme, the proposals for which were often discussed over dinners, with Robin holding court.

I would like to end by thanking Robin for his role in founding the field of research I currently call 'home', and for being a supportive mentor and role model. The event that gave rise to this book involved a number of very stimulating intellectual exchanges. However, I will always remember two things about the occasion. One was the snippet of a memoir that Robin circulated at the outset, in which he intimated he is preparing to 'pass the baton' (see sonnet below). I will always be proud to be one of those taking it up. The other memory of that event will be the photo of Robin on the cover of the programme, because he wore the exact same smile throughout the proceedings. To my mind it is a characteristic expression: laid back, but also piercing, and more than a little bit mischievous.

From Robin to young scholars
Sonnet at seventy

Time for all things meditative
Remembering colleagues I miss
Learning to reminisce
Becoming slow, floppy, vegetative.
From lecture halls with plastic clocks
Drifting thoughts collecting
In minds wirelessly connecting
Threaded through the concrete blocks.

Here's the baton for the young and fitter –
Set aside the lure of money
Drip your minds in Platonic honey
Spray all roads with your knowledge-gritter
Quarry gems from the ivory tower
Unbridle their coruscating power.

17. Living with Difference: From Diaspora to Creolization

Olivia Sheringham

'Creolization is a miracle begging for analysis'
(Michel Trouillot 1998)

My role in the final part of the discussion that we have had over these few days is to talk about creolization, a concept that the Haitian scholar Michel Trouillot described as a 'miracle begging for analysis'. The analysis of this 'miracle' has been central to Robin's work for the best part of a decade, moving on from his remarkable body of work on diaspora, but also drawing out the conceptual and epistemological convergences and divergences between these two terms and the ways in which they are used.

As with diaspora, it seems that *creolization* has been somewhat unleashed and taken into multiple directions in 'semantic, conceptual and disciplinary space' (and here I am quoting Rogers Brubaker).[1] Yet, as with diaspora, Robin has stuck by it, reined it in a bit and contributed some conceptual clout. But he

---

1. Rogers Brubaker, 'The "diaspora" diaspora', *Ethnic and Racial Studies*, vol. 28, 2005, pp. 1–19.

has consistently and coherently hailed the values of creolization for understanding historically and geographically grounded processes of identity formation, as well as possibilities for living with difference in what we might call contemporary contact zones, or 'spaces of encounter'.

I am lucky to have worked with Robin on his most recent project, which is part of the Leverhulme-funded *Oxford Diasporas Programme* (I will not describe the programme in detail as most people here will know to what I am referring).[2] This particular project is called 'Diaspora and creolization: diverging, converging' and it focuses on the social, cultural and historical contexts where creolized and diasporic identities emerge and how they shift over time. It is a comparative project, looking at four different settings, namely Louisiana, Cape Verde, Mauritius and the French Caribbean. As well as analysing secondary literature, we have conducted fieldwork in all these locations – Robin in Louisiana and Mauritius, and me in the French Caribbean and Cape Verde. Moreover, as well as delving into history, we have considered contemporary manifestations of diaspora and creolization through, for example, music, carnival and the construction of heritage.

In this contribution, I shall briefly describe the relationship between creolization and diaspora as we set out to explore it in our project. I will then give some examples from our fieldwork of how these concepts – and social practices associated with them – diverge and converge and mention what we refer to as diasporic pasts and diasporic presents. I shall finish by putting forward three reasons why we feel that creolization could be

---

2. Our research is about to be published in Robin Cohen and Olivia Sheringham, *Encountering difference: diasporic traces, creolizing spaces* (Cambridge: Polity, 2016).

useful, and important, for understanding social identity formations in the twenty-first century.

Diaspora and creolization: diverging, converging

The starting point for this project comes from Robin's
observation of a direct contrast between the concepts of *diaspora*
and *creolization*.

Diaspora (which I will not describe in too much depth as I
know Alan will talk about it) refers broadly to transnational
communities of people dispersed from their homelands.
Originally associated with the Jewish experience, and later with
other forcibly dispersed groups, it involves a link to a historic
past, to a real or imaginary home or homeland that can be
remembered or recreated through contact with tangible people
and places or through acts of the imagination.

Creolization, by contrast, implies a *rupture* with that
original homeland, and denotes the cross-fertilization of two
or more cultural forms as they come together and merge to
create new forms. Creole societies came to refer to those where
old roots are eroded and new languages, people and cultural
practices emerged. In this sense, we can see these two concepts
as representing quite separate 'identity trajectories' (to use
Robin's term), for diaspora's pull to a homeland contrasts with
creolization's creation of something fresh in a new context.

Beyond its original use in linguistics, creolization is clearly
reminiscent of terms like hybridity, *métissage*, *mestizaje*, inter-
culturalism or transculturation, a term coined by the Cuban
anthropologist Fernando Ortiz.[3] However, unlike these related
terms, the 'transculturation' implied within creolization is a

---

3. Fernando Ortiz, *Cuban counterpoint: tobacco and sugar* (Durham: Duke
   University Press, 1995) originally published in Spanish in 1940.

'forced transculturation' (and here I am quoting Stuart Hall), which has its origins in the space of the plantation, in the violent contexts of conquest, colonization and slavery. [4]

Just as there are those who would argue that the term diaspora loses its vigour beyond its association with the Jewish experience, or instances of forced dispersal, for some creolization can *only* be applied to specific historical contexts of violent encounters in the New World. Others, however, *have* taken up the concept as a useful and more widely applicable term to refer to the cross-fertilization of different cultures as they interact. Going even further, people like Ulf Hannerz have used creolization as a more universal metaphor for processes of cultural globalization, suggesting that we live in a 'creolizing world'.

The Martinican writer and thinker, Edouard Glissant also hailed the 'universal values' of the term and suggested that 'perhaps creolization is becoming one of our present-day goals.' Robin's position is that of what you might call a 'cautious proponent' of this more open view. He believes that creolization can be usefully applied to new contexts, but *only* if the differential power relations within such cultural interactions are acknowledged. He is thus mindful of Stuart Hall's warning that, within creolization, 'questions of *power* as well as issues of *entanglement* are always at stake.'[5] Keeping these power dynamics in mind, Robin's work suggests that the concept of creolization gives space to the possibilities for agency, creativity and resistance.

I shall refer to the issue of power later on, but let me now take you on a whirlwind tour of three of the four fieldwork sites

---

4. Stuart Hall, 'Creolization, diaspora, and hybridity in the context of globalization', in Okwui Enwezor et al. (eds) *Créolité and creolization: documenta 11 Platform 3* (Ostfildern-Ruit: Hatje Cantz, 2003) p. 186.
5. Ibid., p. 31.

– Martinique, Cape Verde and Mauritius – and discuss some of our insights into how diaspora and creolization interact with each other.

French Caribbean: creolization, diaspora, metropole

I shall begin in the French Caribbean, the island of Martinique more specifically. Here the relationship between creolized and diasporic identities has taken the form of a kind of cultural politics, led by an astonishing group of writers and intellectuals whose ideas have resonated globally. Here I am referring to people like Franz Fanon, Aimé Césaire and Edouard Glissant (whom I mentioned) to name the most prominent.

A key assertion of diasporic identities took the form of the *Négritude* movement, led by Césaire, who was a poet, writer and later politician. *Négritude* evoked the shared black heritage of the African diaspora and a rejection of French political and intellectual domination. It is important to note that the post-colonial transition of Martinique, and of its neighbouring island Guadeloupe, did not involve independence from France. In fact, it became an overseas department in 1946, so is an integral part of the French *nation*, though the extent to which this differs from a colonial relationship is questionable.

However, to return to *Négritude*, despite its resonance as a key precursor of wider movements for the empowerment of black people, many saw its reassertion of a diasporic identity, rooted in Africa, as unconvincing after three centuries of separation from the continent, centuries marked by extensive cultural mixing or *métissage* through migration, conquest, colonization, slavery and indentured labour. An explicit alternative to *Negritude's* assertion of a diasporic identity came in the form of the *Créolité* movement, which the linguist Jean Bernabé and

169

writers Patrick Chamoiseau and Raphael Confiant founded.[6] In their manifesto for the movement, published in 1989, they announced themselves as 'neither European, nor African, nor Asian, we proclaim ourselves Creoles'[7] and went on to stress that 'we are simultaneously Europe, Africa, enriched by Asian, Levantine and Indian elements, and we also draw from survivals of pre-Colombian America.'

They had been influenced by Glissant who had, in an earlier declaration of Caribbeaness, asserted the heterogeneous and interconnected nature of West Indian identity. Glissant, however, explicitly distanced himself from the *creolité* movement and made a distinction between the *process* of *creolization* and the *state* of creoleness (or *creolité*)

Glissant also, as I mentioned before, saw the value of extending the creolization metaphor *beyond* the Caribbean. For Glissant, the composite nature of Caribbean identity, the creolized spaces that emerged out of traumatic historical experiences, present new ways of thinking about the world, and what he referred to as the relational nature of identities. This way of thinking about creolization as a process is what guided our work on this project.

Beyond these intellectual assertions of difference, of creolized or diasporic identities, we were interested in how they corresponded to the social realities of people in Martinique, how this interaction between creolization and diaspora actually played out on the ground. The Martinican case is a particularly interesting one as it has this added dimension of a pull to the metropole, France, a continual presence of a dominant 'other'.

---

6. M. Giraud, 'Les identites antillaises entre negritude et creolite', *Cahiers des Amériques Latines*, vol. 17, 1994, pp. 141–55.
7. Jean Bernabé, Patrick Chamoiseau and Raphaël Confiant, *Éloge de la créolité* (Paris: Gallimard, 1989) p. 13.

We found several examples of ways in which people defined, defended, performed or lived their identities, which could be associated with creolization or diaspora. In Martinique, I was struck by the revalorization of all things 'creole' in the cultural arena – the creative manifestations of a unique Martinican identity and cultural *difference* from France.

One example is the renewed popularity – among people of all age groups and from different socio-economic backgrounds – of *bélé* – a dance and musical style that emerged during slavery. What were seen as 'African-inspired' dances and drums were prohibited during slavery under the *Code noir,* but Martinicans responded by finding new ways of disguising their dancing – mimicking European square dancing formations – and finding different ways to beat the rhythm.

The French government now provides funds to promote these 'creole' cultural forms as part of concerted efforts to celebrate Martinique's patrimony. In some ways, *bélé* dance can be seen as a kind of nostalgic folklorization of Martinican culture. There is also a sense that these 'traditional' cultural forms are themselves evolving, creolizing and mixing with other cultural influences, including those from new migrant groups that arrive on the island. For several people I interviewed, dance has adapted to shifting social realities on the island, yet *still* represents a manifestation of resistance to French domination. Creole identity in Martinique is not only about a folkloristic, 'top–down' revival of past practices, but also about revisiting and refashioning the past 'from below' as a way of responding to the mystifying past and unpredictable future.

Dance, music and language all provide clear examples of contemporary forms of creolization. Since the 1970s, because of the work of the *creolité* movement, there has been a significant revival and revalorization of Martinican Kréyol (the local language). Efforts to formalize it have included the production of a Kréyol dictionary and the elaboration of a qualification for teaching Kréyol in schools. Alongside the increasing officializ- ation of Kréyol, the creative combinations of Kréyol and French (and sometimes English) among young people continues the trend to creolize 'from below'. In a sense, the linguistic sphere enacts the complex and dynamic identities of these young people, where creoleness and Frenchness at times diverge, but also converge in complex ways.

Cape Verde

I shall turn now to Cape Verde, which is where I did fieldwork (on the island of São Vicente, which is regarded as the more European of the islands), but Robin had done research there on a previous visit, and he went to the island of Santiago (regarded as having closer cultural links to Africa).

Cape Verde was arguably (and here I am citing the historian Toby Green the 'first creole society in the Atlantic world'[8] and became, given its position between Africa, Europe and the Americas, the 'capital of the trans-Atlantic slave trade for the first century'.[9]

It is not surprising that creolized cultural practices and identi- ties emerged in an island nation where there was no possibility for a collective memory of cultural 'roots' before colonization. Nevertheless, despite the undeniably 'creole' nature of Cape Verde and its people, the search for a national identity,

---

8. Tobias Green, 'The evolution of creole identity in Cape Verde', in Robin Cohen and Paola Toninato (eds) *The creolization reader: studies in mixed identities and cultures* (London: Routledge, 2010) pp. 157–66.
9. Ibid.

particularly since independence in 1975, has been marked by contradictions and tensions between Africanness and European-ness, between tradition and modernity. The identity politics in Cape Verde in some ways echoes that of Martinique. There was the cultural and literary movement, *Claridade*, which sought to defend the unique Creole identity of Cape Verde, but where creolization was put forward as an expression of 'cultural Portugueseness'. In contrast to this were the policies of the post-independence government, which aimed to recover the nation's African heritage. Then the subsequent government sought to emphasize the Europeanness of Cape Verdean identity, going as far as to change the country's flag and national anthem to reflect a more European identity.

As well as ignoring the dynamic history of Cape Verde, these discourses of 'authenticity' also disregard the powerful influence of the Cape Verdean diaspora, which, if you include second and third generation emigrants, almost outnumbers those living on the island. The evolution of Cape Verdean identity is therefore *as much* a product of those living there as it is of the diaspora. Elizabeth Challinor, for example, refers to the influence of the Cape Verdean diaspora in these terms: 'if the line between the past and the present were to be drawn differently, then what are perceived as "intrusions" upon Cape Verdean culture may equally be seen as contributions towards the ongoing processes of cultural production.'[10]

Cape Verdean music is illustrative of cultural production both on and off the island in the evolution of Cape Verdean identity. You may well have heard of Cesaria Evora, for example,

---

10. Elizabeth Challinor, *Bargaining in the development market-place: insights from Cape Verde* (Vienna: LIT Verlag, 2005) p. 32.

who brought the musical styles of Morna and the faster paced Coladeira to the global music market. The themes of these styles are often those of departure, Saudade (which means longing), and of double loss – both of original roots and of lives in Cape Verde. A style of Cape Verdean music called *Cabo-Zouk*, which emerged among Cape Verdeans living in France and the Netherlands, is a kind of fusion between French Caribbean Zouk and Cape Verdean rhythms.

It seems that in Cape Verde you cannot talk about the creolization of music without referring to the diaspora. Nonetheless, we found this notion of a diasporic present useful in thinking about the role of the diaspora in the creation of new cultural forms and practices.

The second example I want to give from Cape Verde relates to the carnival, in many ways a creole event, which stages Cape Verde's position at a crossroads between Europe, Africa and the Americas (and my fieldwork happened to coincide with the São Vicente carnival). I wish to mention one figure from it that is illustrative of the cultural entanglements at the heart of Cape Verdean identity. This is the figure of the 'Mandinga', or Mandinka; the term refers to a West African ethnic group, though the meaning has shifted over time. Mandingas at the carnival typically paint their bodies black with a mixture of coal and cooking oil and dance bare-foot in grass skirts, violently shaking a stick bearing a doll's head that is painted black (see photo). The Mandinga, originally a figure that evoked fear and played tricks, traditionally came from the poorest neighbourhoods of São Vicente. The Mandinga's role is *now* primarily to dance and entertain and, as one of my interviewees commented, 'anyone can be a Mandinga'. In many ways, this reflects the more formalized, or commercialized, nature of the Cape Verdean carnival – staged for the enjoyment of tourists.

One could argue that this figure evolved as part of an ongoing process of identity construction in Cape Verde, which expresses changing social realities in the archipelago and involves new processes of creolization as well as the powerful influence of the diaspora. The shifting Mandinga figure – both within and outside the carnival – thus raises interesting questions about Cape Verdean identity in

terms of both its relationship with mainland Africa and the subversive and potentially resistant possibilities that arise through the creative play on this already creolized figure. Mandinga 'parades', which groups of percussionists accompany, now only take place during the official days of the carnival. The photograph of a Mandinga parade was taken on the day that Cape Verde played Ghana in the quarterfinals of the African Cup of Nations.

Mauritius

In Martinique and Cape Verde it seems to be becoming increasingly difficult to separate creolization from diaspora. The links that the people in the vast Cape Verdean diaspora retain with life on the archipelago, and their continual engagement with it, help to create an ongoing process of creolization both there and in their newfound 'homes'. In Mauritius, however, we found more of a *divergence* between creolized and diasporic identities. (I say we, but Robin was the one who conducted the fieldwork in Mauritius last year). Mauritius has been described as a 'textbook case of creolization' for, as Megan Vaughan wrote, 'without natives [it] has always been the product of multiple influences, multiple sources, which to different degrees merge, take root and "naturalize" on this new soil.'

However, we became particularly interested in the construction of heritage as illustrative of a kind of reinvigoration of diasporic identities among different segments of this fundamentally creolized Mauritian society. This reinvigoration of what we refer to as diasporic pasts has come from both the ethnic groups themselves and from their countries of origin. One example is the re-emergence of militant forms of Indian-based religions like the Vishva Hindu Parishad, which serve to solidify ethnic (or diasporic) and religious boundaries.

Another example is in the call for particular places to be recognized as UNESCO world heritage sites. For Indo-Mauritians, this took the form of an immigration depot in Port Louis where nearly half a million Indian indentured labourers landed; it gained recognition as a heritage site in 2006 and was named *Aapravasi Ghat*.

Perhaps in response to this, Mauritians of African-Malagasy origin successfully petitioned for a site known as Le Morne ('the sorrow'), a mountainous area where escaped slaves created Maroon communities, to be recognized as a world heritage site. In this sense, even in what seems to be an archetypal case of creolization, diasporic associations can be 'switched on', responding to shifts in the country of origin, as well as the creol-ized setting, in this case a small island. Yet, this is also illustra-tive of how creolization is not a definitive or one-way process that creates a demarcated 'creole' culture. Rather, these creolized and diasporic identities can be in a continual process of negoti-ation, sometimes reinforcing each other, sometimes diverging.

Conclusion

Now it is time to end, but this is not really a conclusion. Rather, it is more a reflection on an ongoing engagement with the concepts of creolization and diaspora. This paper is really a homage to Robin who has ceaselessly inspired me over the course of this project. We argue that although diaspora and creolization tend in opposite directions – one based around a connection with a past identity or a mythical homeland, the other referring to a severance of past identities and the creation of something new – a closer look at different contexts reveals some possible convergences. I have mentioned the notion of a diasporic past, which refers to the evocation of an original homeland, as in the case of a recent reinvigoration of diasporic links in Mauritius. However, I have also mentioned the case of Cape Verde and what we refer to as a diasporic present. This is the role of the vast Cape Verdean diaspora in the continued processes of creolization – through cultural creativity, for example – both on and off the island.

I said at the beginning that I would propose three key ways in which I think that creolization – mindful of its relationship with diaspora – is useful for analysing identity in the contemporary world, and for addressing some of the challenges of living in ever more super-diverse spaces, for example in today's global cities.

One could sum up these three points as history, space and power. A focus on creolization might compel us to think first about the importance of *history* in the emergence of social and cultural forms and identities; and second about the dynamic relationship between culture and space – from the space of the plantation or island to contemporary contact zones like global cities. Perhaps most importantly, creolization as a concept forces us to recognize socio-economic, gendered and racial *inequalities* – the *power play* that *underlies* many intercultural encounters. Moreover, this is not just about domination and subordination, but it also *necessarily* encompasses creative forms of resistance.

Diaspora and creolization are thus crucial concepts for thinking about identity in our dynamic, ever-more inter-connected world – a world of movement, a world of migrants, a world of 'relation' (to use Edouard Glissant's term). They both represent alternative expressions of identity in the context of forceful assertions of nationalism or religious certain-ties, and challenge the solidity of closed ethnic and racial categories. I would like to finish with a quotation from Robin himself, in which he sums up the progressive possibilities of both creolization and diaspora: 'Expanded uses of diaspora, and certainly creolization, demonstrate that people thrive not by getting stuck in fixed quasi-racial identities but at the nodes and connection points where original ideas and bold inventiveness are nurtured and fashioned.'[11]

---

11. Robin Cohen, 'Social identities, diaspora and creolization', in Kim Knott and Seán McLoughlin (eds) *Diasporas: concepts, identities, intersections* (London: Zed Books, 2010) p. 73.

Appendix

List of Robin Cohen's Publications

> *'Another damned thick, square book! Always scribble, scribble, scribble! Eh Mr. Gibbon?' - The Duke of Gloucester on Edward Gibbon, author of The decline and fall of the Roman Empire.*

AUTHORED and CO-AUTHORED BOOKS

10   *Island societies: collected essays* (Oxford: Oxford Publishing Services ebook, 2016).

9   with Olivia Sheringham, *Encountering difference: diasporic traces, creolizing spaces* (Cambridge: Polity, 2016) 224 pp.

8   *Migration and its enemies: global capital, migrant labour and the nation-state* (Aldershot: Ashgate, 2006) 252 pp.

7   with Paul Kennedy, *Global sociology* (Basingstoke: Macmillan and New York: New York University Press, 2000) 408 pp. (Basingstoke: Palgrave) reprinted 2001, 2002, 2004. Japanese translation 2003. Second expanded and revised edition March 2007 (NYU Press, September 2007). Third edition December 2012. Third US edition, March 2013. Korean translation 2009. Companion website http://www.palgrave.com/sociology/cohen3e/

6   *Global diasporas: an introduction* (London: UCL Press and Seattle: University of Washington Press, 1997) 228 pp. Reprinted 1999, 2000. Reprinted 2001 by Routledge. Japanese translation (Toyko: Akahi Shoten, 2001) by Komai Hiroshi. Greek translation, with new preface, Athens: 2003, 374 pp. Revised second edition London and New York: Routledge, March 2008. Korean translation 2016.

5   *Frontiers of identity: the British and the others* (London: Longman and New York: Addison Wesley, 1994) 248 pp.

4   *Contested domains: debates in international labour studies* (London: Zed Books, 1991) 188 pp.

3   *The new helots: migrants in the international division of labour* (Aldershot: Avebury/Gower Publishing Group, 1987) 290 pp; paperback edition Gower, 1988; Japanese translation, 1989; reprinted 1993, 2003.

2   *Endgame in South Africa: the changing ideology and social structure of South Africa* (Paris: UNESCO Press and London: James Currey 1986) 108 pp; German edition under the title *Endspiel Südafrika: Eine Anatomie der Apartheid* Translated by Ulf Dammann with a Foreword by Jean Ziegler (Berlin: Rotbach Verlag, 1987) 142 pp; US edition (New York: Africa World Press, 1988).

1   *Labour and politics in Nigeria: 1945–71* (London: Heinemann Education Books, 1974, New York: Holmes & Meier/Africana Publishing Corp, 1974). New Heinemann edition with updated introduction and bibliography under the title *Labour and politics in Nigeria*, 1982, 302 pp.

EDITED and CO-EDITED BOOKS

20   with Gunvor Jónsson, *Migration and culture* (Cheltenham: Edward Elgar, 2011) 781 pp.

19   with Paola Toninato, *The creolization reader: studies in mixed identities and cultures* (London and New York: Routledge, 2009) 416 pp.

18   with Steve Vertovec, *Conceiving cosmopolitanism: theory, context and practice* (Oxford and New York: Oxford University Press 2002) 314 pp.

17   with Shirin Rai, *Global social movements* (London: Athlone and New Jersey: Transaction Publishers, 2000) 231 pp [now published by Bloomsbury].

16   with Steve Vertovec, *Migration, diasporas and transnationalism* (Cheltenham: Edward Elgar, 1999) 663 pp.

15   with Zig Layton-Henry, *Politics and migration* (Cheltenham: Edward Elgar, 1998) 341 pp.

14   *Theories of migration* (Cheltenham: Edward Elgar, 1996) 512 pp.

13   *The sociology of migration* (Cheltenham: Edward Elgar, 1996) 544 pp.

12   *Cambridge survey of world migration* (Cambridge: Cambridge University Press, 1995, reprinted in paperback, July 2010) 592 pp.

11   with Harry Goulbourne, *Democracy and socialism in Africa*, (Boulder, CO: Westview Press, 1991 pp. 272.

10   with Abebe Zegeye and Yvonne Muthien, *Repression and resistance: insider accounts of apartheid* (London: Hans Zell Publishers, 1990) 306 pp.

9   with Danièle Joly, *Reluctant hosts: Europe and its refugees*, (Aldershot: Avebury/Gower Publishing Group, 1990, reprinted 1993) 237 pp.

8   with William Cobbett, *Popular struggles in South Africa* (London: James Currey in association with the Review of African Political Economy, 1988; Trenton, New Jersey: Africa World Press, 1988) 234 pp.

180

7　with Peter Gutkind and Rosalind Boyd, *International labour and the third world: the making of a new working class* (Aldershot: Avebury/Gower Publishing Group, 1987) 283 pp.

6　with Fitzroy Ambursley, *Crisis in the Caribbean* (London: Heinemann Educational Books, 1983, New York: Monthly Review Press, 1983, revised edition reprinted 1984) 276 pp.

5　*African islands and enclaves* (Beverly Hills and London: Sage Publications, 1983) 279 pp.

4　with Peter Gutkind and Phyllis Brazier, *Peasants and proletarians: the struggles of third world workers* (London: Hutchinson Books, 1979; New York: Monthly Review Press, 1979) 505 pp.

3　*Forced labour in colonial Africa*, an edition and collection of Albert Nzula's writings (London: Zed Books, 1979) (edited and introduced) 221 pp.

2　with Peter Gutkind and Jean Copans, *African labor history* (Beverly Hills and London: Sage Publications, 1978) 280 pp.

1　with Richard Sandbrook *The development of an African working class: studies in class formation and action* (London: Longman, 1975, Toronto: Toronto University Press, 1976) 330 pp.

PUBLISHED CONFERENCE PROCEEDINGS and SPECIAL ISSUES

3　(©2013) 'Islands, diaspora and creolization', *Diaspora: A Journal of Transnational Studies* (guest-edited by Robin Cohen and Olivia Sheringham). Issue backdated 17, no. 1, 2008, 124 pp.

2　(2006) A selection of papers below published as a special issue (guest editor, Robin Cohen) similarly titled 'Migration and health in southern Africa', *Journal of Ethnic and Migration Studies*, 32, no. 4, May 2006, 181 pp.

1　(2003) *Migration and Health in Southern Africa*. Proceedings of a conference held at the University of Cape Town, 26–9 January 2003. Contributions by 21 authors, perfect bound in A4 size by Van Schaik Content Solutions, Stellenbosch, South Africa, 236 pp.

MAJOR ARTICLES and CHAPTERS in EDITED COLLECTIONS

66　with Nicholas Van Hear, 'Diasporas and conflict', *Oxford Development Studies*, forthcoming 2016.

65　'Reconsidering social inclusion/exclusion in social theory: nine perspectives, three levels', *Mondi Migranti: Rivista di studi e ricerche sulle migrazioni internazionali* (Franco Angelli), Issue 1, 2015, pp. 7–29.

64　with Olivia Sheringham, 'The salience of islands in the articulation of creolization and diaspora', *Diaspora: a journal of transnational studies*, vol. 17, no. 1, 2008, pp. 6–17, © 2013.

Appendix

63   with Gunvor Jónsson, 'Connecting culture and migration', Introduction to Robin Cohen and Gunvor Jónsson (eds) *Migration and culture* (Cheltenham: Edward Elgar, 2011) pp. xiii–xxxii.

62   with Lesley Marx, 'Cinematic representations of diaspora: Italians and Jews', *Crossings: Journal of Migration and Culture*, vol. 1, no. 1, 2010, pp. 5–23.

61   with Paola Toninato, 'The creolization debate: analysing mixed identities and cultures' in Robin Cohen and Paola Toninato (eds) *The creolization reader: studies in mixed identities and cultures* (London: Routledge, 2009) pp. 1–22.

60   'Solid, ductile and liquid: the changing role of homeland and home in diaspora studies', in Y. Sternberg and E. Ben Rafael (eds) *Transnationalism: diasporas and the advents of a new dis(order)*, (Leiden: Brill, 2009) pp. 117–34.

59   'Sólidas, dúcteis e líquida: noções em mutação de "lar" e "terra natal" nos estudios da diaspora', *Caderno CRH, Salvador*, vol. 21, no. 54, September–December 2008, pp. 519–32.

58   'Creolization and diaspora: the cultural politics of divergence and (some) convergence', in Gloria Totoricagüena (ed.) *Opportunity structures in diaspora relations: comparisons in contemporary multi-level politics of diaspora and transnational identity* (Reno, Nevada, Center for Basque Studies, University of Nevada Press, 2008) pp. 85–112.

57   'Creolization and cultural globalization: the soft sounds of fugitive power', *Globalizations*, vol. 4, no. 3, September 2007, pp. 369–84.

56   'The free movement of people: ethical debates before and after 9/11', in Christine Chinkin, David Downes, Conor Gearty and Paul Rock (eds) *Sociology and politics of denial: crime, social control and human rights – Essays in honour of Stanley Cohen* (Cullompton, Devon: Willan Publishing, 2007) pp. 211–25.

55   'Diasporas: changing meanings and limits of the concept', in William Berthomière and Christine Chivallon (eds) *Les diasporas dans le monde contemporain* (Paris: Karthala and Maison des Sciences de l'Homme, Bordeaux, Pessac, 2006) pp. 39–48.

54   'La liberté de circulation de devises et de personnes: les débats avant et après le 11 Septembre 2001', *Migrations Société*, vol. 27, no. 102, November–December 2005, pp. 45–69.

53   'Globalização, migração international e cosmopolitismo quotidiano', in António Barreto (ed.) *Globalizaçõao e migraçõoes* (Lisboa: Instituto Ciencias Sociais, 2005) pp. 25–43.

52   'Reti di migranti transnazionali', in Maddalena Tirabassi (ed.) *Itinera: paradigmi delle migrazioni italiane* (Turin: Edizioni della Fondazione Giovanni Agnelli, 2005) pp. 21–42.

51   'Chinese cockle-pickers, the transnational turn and everyday cosmopolitanism: reflections on the new global migrants', *Labour, Capital and Society*, vol. 37, no. 2, 2004, pp. 130–49.

50   with Steven Vertovec, 'Introduction: conceiving cosmopolitanism', in S. Vertovec and R. Cohen (eds) *Conceiving cosmopolitanism: theory, context and practice* (Oxford: Oxford University Press, 2002) pp. 1–22.

49   with Robert Fine, 'Four cosmopolitan moments', in Steven Vertovec and Robin Cohen (eds) *Conceiving cosmopolitanism: theory, context and practice* (Oxford: Oxford University Press, 2002) pp. 137–62.

48   'Labour in an age of global insecurity', in Barbara Harriss-White (ed.) *Globalization and insecurity: political, economic and physical challenges* (Basingstoke: Palgrave, 2001) pp. 203–17.

47   with Shirin Rai, 'Global social movements: towards a cosmopolitan politics', in Robin Cohen and Shirin M. Rai (eds) *Global social movements* (London: Athlone and New Jersey: Transaction Books, 2000) pp. 1–17.

46   'Introduction', in S. Vertovec and R. Cohen (eds) *Migration, diasporas and transnationalism* (Cheltenham: Edward Elgar, 1999) pp. xiii–xxviii.

45   'Back to the future: from metropolis to cosmopolis', in Jan Hjarnø (ed.) *From metropolis to cosmopolis* (Esbjerg, Denmark: South Jutland University Press, 1999) pp. 9–26.

44   'L'alieno come construzione sociale: sette teorie dell'esclusione', in Marcella Della Donne (ed.) *Relazioni etniche: stereotypipi e preguidizi* (Rome: EdUP, 1998) pp. 47–61.

43   'Cultural diasporas: the Caribbean case', in Mary Chamberlain (ed.) *Global identities* (London: Routledge, 1998) pp. 21–35.

42   'Shaping the nation, excluding the other: the deportation of migrants from Britain', in Leo Lucassen and Jan Lucassen (eds) *Migration, migration history, history, old paradigms and new perspectives* (Bern: Peter Lang AG Europäishcer Verlag der Wissenschaften, 1997) pp. 351–73.

41   'Diasporas, the nation-state and globalisation', in Wang Gungwu (ed.) *Global history and migrations* (Boulder, CO: Westview, 1997) pp. 117–43.

40   'Diasporas and the nation-state: from victims to challengers', *International Affairs* vol. 72, no. 3, July 1996, pp. 507–20.

39   'Fuzzy frontiers of identity: the British case', *Social Identities*, vol 1, no. 1, January 1995, pp. 35–62.

38   'Rethinking Babylon: iconoclastic conceptions of the diaspora experience', *New Community*, vol. 21, no. 1, January 1995, pp. 5–18.

37   'La diaspora d'une diaspora: le cas des Antilles', in R. Gallissot (ed.) *Pluralisme cultural en Europe* (Paris: L'Harmattan, 1993) pp. 61–77.

36   'Race and ethnicity in a post-apartheid society: "pluralism" revisited', in Herminio Martins (ed.) *Knowledge and passion: essays in honour of John Rex* (London: I.B.Tauris, 1993) pp. 1–22.

35   'A diaspora of a diaspora? The case of the Caribbean', *Social Science Information*, vol. 31, no. 1, 1992, pp. 193–203.

Appendix

34 'Migration and the new international division of labour', in Malcolm Cross (ed.) *Ethnic minorities and industrial change in Europe and North America* (Cambridge: Cambridge University Press, 1991) pp. 19–35.

33 'European and East-West migration in a global context', *New Community*, vol. 17, no. 4, October 1991, pp. 9–26.

32 'Democracy or socialism, democracy and socialism', in Robin Cohen and Harry Goulbourne (eds) *Democracy and socialism in Africa* (Boulder, CO: Westview Press, 1991) pp. 1–12.

31 with Yvonne Muthien and Abebe Zegeye, 'Introduction', in R. Cohen et al., *Resistance and repression: insider accounts of apartheid* (London: Hans Zell, 1990) pp. 1–16.

30 'Citizens, denizens and helots: the politics of international migration flows in the post-war world', *Hitotsubashi Journal of Social Studies*, vol. 21, no. 1, August 1989, pp. 153–65.

29 with D. Joly, 'Introduction: the "new refugees" of Europe', in D. Joly and R. Cohen (eds) *Reluctant hosts: Europe and its refugees* (Aldershot: Avebury/Gower Publishing Group, 1989) pp. 5–18.

28 'The detention of asylum-seekers in the UK', in D. Joly and R. Cohen (eds) *Reluctant hosts: Europe and its refugees* (Aldershot: Avebury/ Gower Publishing Group, 1989) pp. 145–61.

27 'An academic perspective' [to the book's theme], in C. Clarke and T. Payne (eds) *Politics, development and security in small states* (London: Allen & Unwin, 1988) pp. 203–13.

26 'Popular struggles or one struggle: dilemmas of liberation', in W. Cobbett and R. Cohen (eds) *Popular struggles in South Africa* (London: James Currey, 1988) pp. 1–19.

25 'Theorising international labour', in R. Boyd, R. Cohen and P. C. W. Gutkind (eds) *International labour and the third world* (Aldershot: Avebury/Gower Publishing Group, 1987) pp. 3–25.

24 '"A greater South" a reinterpretation of the prelude to the Nigerian civil war', *Manchester Papers on Development*, vol. 3, no. 3, November 1987, pp. 1–24.

23 'Policing the frontiers: the state and the migrant in the international division of labour', in J. Henderson and M. Castells (eds) *Global restructuring and territorial development* (London: Sage, 1987) pp. 88–111.

22 'The "new" international division of labour: a conceptual, historical and empirical critique', *Migration: a European Journal of Migration & Ethnic Relations*, vol. 1, no. 1, July 1987, pp. 22–40.

21 'Marxism in Africa: the grounding of a tradition', in B. Munslow (ed.) *Africa: problems in the transition to socialism* (London: Zed, 1986) pp. 40–55.

20 'Policing the frontiers: regulating the supplies of migrant labour', *Manchester Papers on Development* (New Series) vol. 1, no. 3, November 1985, pp. 1–29.

19 'Education for dependence: aspirations, expectations and identity on the island of St Helena', *Manchester Papers in Development*, no. 8, November 1983, pp. 1–30.

18 with Fitzroy Ambursley, 'The crisis of the state in the Caribbean', in F. Ambursley and R. Cohen (eds) *Crisis in the Caribbean* (London: Heinemann and New York: Monthly Review Press, 1983) pp. 1–26.

17 'Introduction', in R. Cohen (ed.) *African islands and enclaves* (Beverly Hills: Sage Publications, 1983) pp. 9–19.

16 'St Helena: welfare colonialism in practice', in R. Cohen (ed.) *African islands and enclaves* (Beverly Hills: Sage, 1983) pp. 119–44.

15 with Jeff Henderson, 'On the reproduction of the relations of production', in R. Forrest et al. (eds) *Urban political economy and social theory* (Aldershot: Gower Publications, 1982) pp. 112–43.

14 with Jeff Henderson, 'Work, culture and the dialectics of proletarian habituation', *Papers in Urban & Regional Studies*, no. 3, 1980, pp. 3–34.

13 'Resistance and hidden forms of consciousness amongst African workers', *Review of African Political Economy*, vol. 7, no. 19, September–December 1980, pp. 8–22.

12 'Albert Nzula: the road from Rouxville to Russia', in Belinda Bozzoli (ed.) *Labour, townships & protest* (Johannesburg: Ravan Press, 1979) pp. 325–40.

11 'Michael Imoudu et l'essor du syndicalisme au Nigeria', in C. A. Julian et al. (eds) *Les Africains* (Paris: Jeune Afrique, vol. 10, 1978) pp. 177–205.

10 with Arnold Hughes, 'Identity and protest in the Lagos proletariat, 1897–1939', in P. C. W. Gutkind, R. Cohen and J. Copans (eds) *African labor history* (Beverly Hills: Sage Publications, 1978) pp. 31–55.

9 'The politics of unemployment in Mauritius', *Manpower & Unemployment Research*, vol. 11, no. 1, April 1978, pp. 3–18.

8 'The making of a West African working class', in T. Shaw and K. Heard (eds) *The politics of Africa: dependence and development* (London: Longman/New York: Africana Publishing Corporation, 1978) pp. 5–21.

7 with Teodor Shanin and Bernado Sorj, 'The sociology of developing societies: problems of teaching and definition', *Sociological Review*, vol. 25, no. 2, May 1977, pp. 351–75.

6 'Michael Imoudu and the Nigerian labour movement', *Race & Class*, vol. 18, no. 4, Spring 1977, pp. 345–62.

5 'From peasants to workers in Africa', in P. C. W. Gutkind and I. Wallerstein (eds) *The political economy of contemporary Africa* (Beverly Hills: Sage Publications, 1976) pp. 155–68.

4 with Caroline Hutton, 'African peasants and resistance to change: a reconsideration of sociological approaches', in D. Booth et al. (eds) *Beyond the sociology of development* (London: Routledge & Kegan Paul, 1975) pp. 105–30.

Appendix

3   with Roy May, 'The interaction between race and colonialism: a case study of the Liverpool race riots of 1919', *Race & Class*,vol. 16, no. 2, October 1974, pp. 111–26.

2   'Class in Africa: analytical problems and perspectives', in R. Miliband and J. Saville (eds) *The Socialist Register* (London: Merlin Press, 1972) pp. 231–55. Available online at http://socialist register.com

1   'Further comments on the Kilby/Weeks debate', *Journal of Developing Areas*, vol. 5, no. 2, January 1971, pp. 155–64.

OTHER PUBLICATIONS

(includes short articles, review articles, translations, selected reprints and online publications)

126   with Joanna Story, 'The impact of diasporas', Foreword to Robin Cohen and Joanna Story with Nicholas Moon (eds) *The Impact of Diasporas*, Oxford Diasporas Programme, University of Oxford and the Impact of Diasporas programme, University of Leicester, September 2015, pp. 5–6.

125   'Seeds, roots, rhizomes and epiphytes: botany and diaspora', in Alan Gamlen, Nando Sigona, Giulia Liberatore and Heléne Neveu-Kingelbach (eds) *Diasporas reimagined* (Oxford: Oxford Diasporas Programme, University of Oxford, 2015) pp. 2–7.

124   'Diasporas, conceptually speaking', Foreword to Alan Gamlen, Nando Sigona, Giulia Liberatore and Heléne Neveu-Kingelbach (eds) *Diasporas reimagined* (Oxford: Oxford Diasporas Programme, University of Oxford, 2015) pp. xv–xvi.

123   'Refugia: the limits and possibilities of Buzi's refugee nation', postcards from, 30 July 2015: https://nandosigona.wordpress.com/2015/07/30/refugia-the-limits-and-possibilities-of-buzis-refugee-nation/

122   with Nicholas Van Hear, 'Diasporas and conflict', Working Paper, Oxford Diasporas Programme and Centre on Migration, Policy and Society, University of Oxford, WP-15-122, 2015, 21 pp.

121   'More Farage, more immigration', published online in *Discover Society*, February 2015, http://www.discoversociety.org/2015/02/ 01/more-farage-more-immigration/

120   'For creolization, against diaspora, interlacing both', review article for *Diasporas: A Journal of Diaspora Studies*, vol. 18, no. 3, pp. 413–20 © 2015

119   'Foreword', in Daniel Conway and Pauline Leonard, *Migration, space and transnational identities: the British in South Africa* (London: Palgrave Macmillan, 2014) pp. vi–vii.

118   'Interview on mechanisms of identity construction in diasporas', *New Literary Observer* (*Novoe literaturnoe obozrenie*), Moscow, no. 127, September 2014.

117 'Foreword', Gurminder Bhambra, *Connecting sociologies* (London: Bloomsbury, 2014).

116 'Stuart Hall: a memoir and a tribute', *Network: A Newsletter of the British Sociological Association*, no. 116, 2014, pp. 22–3.

115 'Migration and culture', in Michael Keith and Bridget Anderson (eds) *Ten years of migration studies: an anthology* (Centre on Migration, Policy and Society, University of Oxford, 2014) pp. 73–5.

114 'Creolization in rural Louisiana', photo essay as part of a creolization and diaspora project, 2013 http://www.migration.ox.ac.uk/odp/creolization-in-louisiana-photo-essay.shtml#&panel1-1

113 with Olivia Sheringham, 'Quotidian creolization and diasporic echoes: resistance and co-optation in Cape Verde and Louisiana', Working Paper, no. 72, International Migration Institute, University of Oxford, July 2013, 30 pp.

112 with Olivia Sheringham, 'Introduction: islands and identities', *Diaspora: A Journal of Transnational Studies*, vol. 17, no. 1, 2008, pp. 1–5, © 2013.

111 'Robin Cohen and Khachig Tölölyan discuss diasporas', video, http://vimeo.com/25020401 2012, 16 min.

110 'Alan Gamlen interviews Robin Cohen about the concept of diaspora', video, http://vimeo.com/37177848, 2012, 37 minutes.

109 with Lesley Marx. 'Cinematic representations of diaspora: Italians and Jews', in Robin Cohen and Gunvor Jónsson (eds) *Migration and culture* (Cheltenham: Edward Elgar, 2011) pp. 185–203.

108 'On the move: the migration imperative', *Global*, no. 5, January 2011, an online magazine published in association with the Commonwealth Secretariat. Available from http://www.global-briefing.org/2011/01/on-the-move-the-migration-imperative/

107 'Emphatic beginnings: from culture contact to creolization', online contribution (Max Planck Institute for the Study of Religious and Ethnic Diversity) http://www.mmg.mpg.de/special-output/blogs/cohen-emphatic-beginnings-october-2010/

106 'Foreword to Laurent Medea, *Réunion: an island in search of an identity* (Pretoria: Unisa and Bordeaux: University of Bordeaux, 2010) pp. xix–xxi.

105 'Social identities, diaspora and creolization', in Kim Knott and Seán McLoughlin (eds) *Diasporas: concepts, identities, intersections* (London: Zed Books, 2010) pp. 69–73.

104 'Interview with Robin Cohen on "The law of success"', blog created by Haegwan Kim, http://lawofsuccess2.blogspot.com/2010/05/ interview-with-robin-cohen.html, 2010.

103 'Interview with Robin Cohen on the idea of diversity', *Max Planck Institute for Ethnic and Religious Diversity*, http://www.mmg.mpg.de/english/Special_output/Interviews/Cohen_2010/index.html, 2010.

102 'Towards a post credit-crunch politics: restoring a grand narrative', online comment, *The Broker,* posted 28 October 2008, http://www.thebrokeronline.eu/en/Debate/Deep-democracy

101 'Brain drain migration', in Rashmi Ingle (ed.) *Globalization, economic development and brain drain* (Pune, India: ICFAI University Press, February 2008) reprint.

100 'Preface', in Isabel Estrada Carvalais, *Postnational citizenship and the state: the political integration of non-national residents in Portugal* (Lisbon: Celta Editora, 2007) pp. ix–x.

99 'Solid, ductile and liquid: the changing role of homeland and home in diaspora studies', Queen Elizabeth House, Working Paper, no. 156, 2007, pp. 1–17. http://www3.qeh.ox.ac.uk/pdf/qehwp/qehwps156.pdf

98 'Dismantling the heritage of apartheid in South Africa's universities', *Indira Management Review,* vol. 1, no. 1, February 2007, pp. 31–9.

97 'Creolization', in George Ritzer (ed.) *The Blackwell encyclopaedia of sociology* (Malden, MA: Blackwell, 2007) pp. 817–18.

96 'Diaspora and migration', in John Scott (ed.) *Sociology: the key concepts* (London: Routledge, 2006) pp. 103–4.

95 'Introduction: from fear to solidarity', in Robin Cohen (guest editor) *Migration and health in southern Africa,* special issue of *Journal of Ethnic and Migration Studies,* vol. 32, no. 4, May 2006, pp. 561–7.

94 '"Diaspora": changing meanings and limits of the concept', in John LaGuerre and Ann Marie Bissessar (eds) *Calcutta to Caroni and the Indian Diaspora,* St Augustine, Trinidad and Tobago: The University of the West Indies, School of Continuing Studies, 2005, pp. 39–48.

93 'Preface' to Chan Kwok Bun, *Migration, ethnic relations and Chinese business* (London Routledge, 2005) pp. xi–xii.

92 'Diaspora, the nation-state and globalization', in Bruce Mazlish and Akira Iriye (eds) *The global history reader* (New York: Routledge, 2005) pp. 92–103, reprinted.

91 'Migration', in Adam Kuper and Jessica Kuper (eds) *The social science encyclopedia* (London: Routledge, 2004) reprinted 2008.

90 'Il mondo delle diaspore ci fa paura', *Reset* (Rome), vol. 84, July–August 2004, pp. 75–8.

89 'Quella ebraica, madre di tutti le diaspore', *Reset* (Rome), vol. 82, March–April 2004, pp. 44–8.

88 with Paul Kennedy, New 'Introduction' to the 2 vol. Japanese edition of *Global sociology* (Tokyo, 2003).

87 '"Diaspora": beyond the Jewish experience', 15th Jacob Gitlin public memorial lecture at the Jacob Gitlin Memorial Library, Albow Centre, Cape Town, South Africa, 18 September, 2003, pamphlet published by the Gitlin Library, library location JGML 12, ISBN: 0-620-31368-4, pp. 1–11.

86   'Introduction: from fear to solidarity', in *Migration and health in Southern Africa* Proceedings of a conference held at the University of Cape Town, 26–9 January 2003. Van Schaik Content Solutions, Stellenbosch, South Africa, 2003, pp. 1–7, available at www.csol.co.za.

85   'Preface' to the Greek edition of *Global diasporas: an introduction* Athens, 2003, pp. 21–4.

84   'Crossing the line. Migration: the end of borders', *Index on Censorship*, vol. 32, no. 2, May 2003, pp. 60–9.

83   'Diaspora', in Neil J. Smelser and Paul B. Baltes (editors-in-chief) *International encyclopaedia of the social and behavioral sciences* (Oxford: Pergamon, 2001) pp. 3642–5.

82   with Alisdair Rogers and Steve Vertovec, 'Editorial statement' in the opening issue of *Global Networks*, vol. 1, no. 1, 2001, pp. iii–vi.

81   'The diaspora of a diaspora: the Caribbean case', in Harry Goulbourne (ed.) *Race and ethnicity: critical concepts in sociology*, vol. 2, *Solidarities and communities* (London: Routledge, 2001) reprinted from *Social Science Information*, vol. 31, no. 1, 1992, pp. 193–203).

80   'Fuzzy frontiers of identity: the British case', in Harry Goulbourne (ed.) *Race and ethnicity: critical concepts in sociology*, vol. 2, *Solidarities and communities* (London: Routledge, 2001) reprinted from *Social Identities*, vol. 1, no. 1, January 1995, pp. 35–62.

79   'European and East–West migration in a global context', in Malcolm Cross (ed.) *The sociology of race and ethnicity* (Cheltenham: Edward Elgar, 2001) reprinted from *New Community* vol. 17, no. 4, 1991, pp. 9–26.

78   'The incredible vagueness of being British/English', *International Affairs*, vol. 76, no. 3, 2000, pp. 575–82 (review article).

77   'Migration and identity', public lecture supported by the Immigration History Research Center, University of Minnesota, Minneapolis, 21 October 1999 Audiotape of lecture and question/answer session (90 minutes).

76   'The making of ethnicity: a modest defence of primordialism', in Edward Mortimer and Robert Fine (eds) *People, nation and state* (London: I.B.Tauris, 1999) pp. 3–11.

75   'Migration and international politics: new forms, new sensitivities', in *Masses on the move: migration and international politics*, Summary record of a seminar series, Foreign Policy Studies Programme, All Souls College, University of Oxford, Hilary Term 1999 (convenors Julian Bullard and Robert O' Neill) pp. 1–19.

74   'Diasporas and the nation-state: from victims to challengers', *International Affairs*, vol. 72, no. 3, July 1996, pp. 507–20, reprinted in S. Vertovec and R. Cohen (eds) *Migration, diasporas and transnationalism* (Cheltenham: Edward Elgar, 1999) pp. 266–79.

73   Rethinking Babylon: iconoclastic conceptions of the diaspora experience', *New Community*, vol. 21, no. 1, January 1995, pp. 5–18,

reprinted in S. Vertovec and R. Cohen (eds) *Migration, diasporas and transnationalism* (Cheltenham: Edward Elgar, 1999) pp. 252–65.

72 'Transnational social movements: an assessment', 1998. Working Papers on Transnational Communities (WPTC 98-09), posted at www.transcomm.ox.ac.uk

71 'Diasporas and the nation-state: from victims to challengers', *International Affairs*, vol. 72, no. 3, July 1996, pp. 507–20, reprinted in David Graham and Nana Poku (eds) *Redefining security: population movements and national security* (Westport, CN: Praeger, 1998) pp. 51–66.

70 'Introduction', in Robin Cohen and Zig Layton-Henry (eds) *The politics of migration* (Cheltenham: Edward Elgar, 1997) pp. ix–xvi.

69 'Trades unions and associations', in J. Middleton (ed.) *The encyclopaedia of Africa: south of the Sahara* (New York: Simon and Schuster, 1997) pp. 101–3.

68 'Introduction', in Robin Cohen (ed.) *The sociology of migration* (Cheltenham: Edward Elgar, 1996) pp. xi–xvii.

67 'Introduction', in Robin Cohen (ed.) *Theories of migration* (Cheltenham: Edward Elgar, 1996) pp. xi–xvii.

66 'European and East-West migration in a global context', *New Community*, vol. 17, no. 4, October 1991, pp. 9–26, reprinted in Colin Holmes (ed.) *European history and migration* (Cheltenham: Edward Elgar, 1996) pp. 13–30.

65 'International migration and the future of the nation-state', *New Community*, vol. 22, no. 1, 1996, pp. 159–63 (review article).

64 *Global Diasporas Project*. Material relating to this project, including a very large bibliography, is available on www.warwick.ac.uk (follow the route from this home page via 'Faculties' to 'Departments' to 'Sociology' to 'Global Diasporas Project') Bibliography also posted at www.transcomm.ox.ac.uk

63 'International migration: South Africa in global perspective', in J. Crush and F. Veriava (eds) *Transforming South Africa's immigration policy* (Kingston, Ontario: Southern African Migration Project, 1997).

62 'Brain drain migration', in J. Crush and F. Veriava (eds) *Transforming South Africa's immigration policy* (Kingston, Ontario: Southern African Migration Project, 1997) pp. 46–52. Also posted at www.queensu.ca/samp/transform/Cohen1.htm

61 'La diaspora di una diaspora: il caso delle Antille', in René Gallissot and Annamaria Rivera (eds) *Pluralismo culturale in Europa* (Rome: Edizioni Dedalo, 1995) pp. 49–62.

60 'Preface', in Marcella Della Donne (ed.) *Avenues to integration: refugees in contemporary Europe* (Naples: Ipermedium, 1995) pp. 1–2.

59 'Migration', in E. Ellis Cashmore (ed.) *Dictionary of race and ethnic relations* (London: Routledge, 1994, 3rd edition) pp. 210–14.

58 'Expansion and quality' [in Higher Education], *The New Academic*, vol. 3, no. 1, 1994, pp. 1–3.

57 'The broken-backed state and uncivil society', foreword to R. Deosaran, *A society under siege: a study of political confusion and legal mysticism* (Port of Spain, Trinidad: Tex Publishing Company and The Caribbean Institute for Human Rights, 1993) pp. vii–xii.

56 'A death too far: deportations from the UK', *New Statesman & Society*, 13 August 1993, p. 17.

55 'Migrants in Europe: processes of exclusion and inclusion', *New Community*, vol. 18, no. 2, 1992, pp. 332–36 (review article).

54 'Race and ethnicity in a post-apartheid society: "pluralism" revisited', translated into German as 'Ethnizität in Südafrika der Apartheid: Zum Begriff "Pluralismus"', *Jahrbuch für Vergleichende Sozialforschung* (Berlin: Berliner Institut für Vergleichende Sozialforschung in der Arbeitsgemeinschaft Europsäiches Migrationszentrum, Band 5, July 1992) pp. 11–36.

53 'Bürger, Eingebürgerte und Heloten: Zur Politik der internationalen Migrationsbewegun in der Nachkriegszeit', in Jochen Blaschke and Andreas Germeshausen (eds) *Sozialwissenschaftliche Studien Über das Weltdflüchtingsproblem* (Band 1, Berlin: Edition Parabolis, 1992) pp. 53–74.

52 'Reiche Länder brauchen Gepäckträger', *Die Tageszeitung* (Berlin) 8 June 1991, pp. 54–6 (syndicated to 18 newspapers worldwide).

51 'Foreword', in R. Munck, *The new international labour studies: an introduction* (London: Zed Books, 1988) pp. ix–xi.

50 'The effects of the Immigration Act of 1988 on race relations', in Birmingham Community Relations Council, *Report and recommendations of the conference on the implications of the Immigration Act of 1988 held on 10 October, 1988* (Birmingham: CRC, 1988) pp. 11–12.

49 'Employment, ethnic relations and the media: concluding comments', in J. Harte (ed.) *Race and employment in the media* (London: Commission for Racial Equality and the London Borough of Lewisham, 1988) pp. 110–18.

48 with Carolyn Baylies, 'Editorial', *Review of African Political Economy*, no. 39, 1987, pp. 1–3.

47 'Les formes cachées de la résistance et de la conscience ouvrières', in M. Agier, J. Copans and A. Morice (eds) *Classes ouvrières d'Afriques noire* (Paris: Karthala, 1987) pp. 113–36.

46 'Monologue and dialogue in international labour studies', *Canadian Review of Sociology & Anthropology*, vol. 23, no. 1, February 1986, pp. 150–6 (review article).

45 'Foreword' to reissued book by Ken Pryce, *Endless pressure* (Bristol: Bristol Classical Press, 1986) pp. xv–xxi.

Appendix

44 with Carolyn Baylies and Gavin Williams, 'Editorial' for an issue title 'The struggle for spoils', *Review of African Political Economy*, vol. 13, no. 35, Spring 1986, pp. 1–3.

43 'Some theories of migration: a synopsis and comment', in A. L. Gustavson and T. Sachs (eds) *Themes and theories in migration research* (Copenhagen: Danish Social Science Research Council, 1986) pp. 1–11.

42 'Living with dependence: a Caribbean lament', *Journal of Development Studies*, vol. 21, no. 3, April 1985, pp. 458–63 (review article).

41 'Preface', in D Bolton, *Nationalisation: a road to socialism?* (London: Zed Books, 1985) pp. xi–xii.

40 'Sociology and development literature: a critical overview', Discussion Paper No. 26, Centre for Developing Area Studies, *McGill University*, 1985, 17 pp.

39 'Les nouvelles etudes sur le travail à l'échelle internationale', *Travail et travailleurs de la tiers monde* (Bulletin d'information et de liaison, ORSTOM and EHESS, Paris, November 1984) pp. 12–21.

38 'Development strategies in the Caribbean with particular reference to socialist countries', in R. Ploeg (ed.) *What you should know about the Caribbean* (Leiden: Royal Institute of Linguistics & Anthropology, 1984).

37 'Preface', in J. Crisp, *The story of an African working class: Ghanaian miners' struggles, 1870–1980* (London: Zed Books, 1984) pp. xvi–xviii.

36 'The sociology of development and the development of sociology', *Social Science Teacher*, vol. 12, no. 2, Spring 1983, pp. 52–7.

35 with Jeff Henderson, 'Den internationale restrukturering of kapital og arbeid', in A. Wangel (ed.) *Sociologi: internationale arbeidsstudies* (Copenhagen) vol. 1, no. 1, 1983, pp. 14–45.

34 'Unmaking Grenada's revolution', *New Society*, vol. 66, no. 1094, 3 November 1983, pp. 196–7.

33 with Peter Lawrence, 'Editorial' for 'Tribute to Ruth First', *Review of African Political Economy*, vol. 9, no. 25, Winter 1982, pp. 1–4.

32 'Workers in developing societies', in H. Alavi and T. Shanin (eds) *Introduction to the sociology of developing societies* (London: Macmillan and New York: Monthly Review Press, 1982) pp. 279–86.

31 'Hidden forms of protest' and 'From peasants to workers', Extracts from earlier articles in G. Williams and C. H. Allen (eds) *The sociology of developing societies: sub-Saharan Africa* (London: Macmillan and New York: Monthly Review Press, 1982).

30 'Resistance and hidden forms of consciousness among African workers', in Hazel Johnson and Henry Bernstein (eds) *Third world lives of struggle* (London: Heinemann Educational Books for the Open University, 1982) pp. 244–58 (reprint).

29 'Althusser meets Anancy: structuralism and popular protest in Ken Post's history of Jamaica', *Sociological Review*, May 1982, pp. 345–57 (review article).

28 'Introduction to second impression', in R. Cohen, *Labour and politics in Nigeria* (London: Heinemann, 1982) pp. viii–xv.

27 'Reply to Eddie Webster', Debate section, *Review of African Political Economy*, vol. 8, no. 22, Winter 1981, pp. 101–2.

26 'The end to the migrant labour boom', *Newsletter on International Labour Studies*, no. 10, April 1981, pp. 1–6.

25 'Migrants on the screen and in the theatre', *Newsletter on International Labour Studies*, no. 10, April 1981, pp. 24–6.

24 'Introduction to section on "race and class"', in S. Craig (ed.) *Contemporary Caribbean: a sociological reader* (Maracas, Trinidad: The College Press, 1981) pp. 187–9.

23 'Wales: a suitable case of combined and uneven development?' *Sociology in Wales*, vol. 4, no. 4, 1981, pp. 7–10 (review article).

22 with Pepe Roberts and Morris Szeftel, 'Editorial for issue on 'Peasants, Capital and the State', *Review of African Political Economy*, vol. 8, no. 21, May–September 1981, pp. 1–6.

21 'Trade unionism and industrial relations in Trinidad and Tobago', *Annuario Sindical Abierto* (Mexico City: Instituto Nacional de Estudios de Trabajo and Centro de Estudios Sociólogicos, El Colégio de México, 1979) 24 pp.

20 with Jeff Henderson, 'Capital and the work ethic', *Monthly Review*, vol. 31, no. 6, November 1979, pp. 11–26.

19 with co-editors, 'Introduction', in P. C. W. Gutkind, R. Cohen and J. Copans (eds) *African labor history* (Beverly Hills: Sage Publications, 1978) pp. 7–30.

18 'Preface', in R. Deosaran, 'Collected papers on carnival, race, prejudice and the politics of Trinidad', Working Papers on Caribbean Society, *University of the West Indies* Series C, no. 3, August 1978.

17 'Basil Davidson's Africa', *West Africa*, January 1977 (review article).

16 with Samir Amin, *Classes and class struggle in Africa*, pamphlet published by Afrografika Publishers, Yaba, Nigeria 1977, 56 pp. Note: this is a pirate edition of Cohen 'Class in Africa…' (1972), together with colourful and bogus biographical sketches of the authors.

15 with Robert Poulton, 'Contemporary communes: a bibliographical and interpretative essay', Discussion Paper Series C, no. 31, Faculty of Commerce and Social Science, *University of Birmingham*, June 1977, 33 pp.

14 Various short articles and entries on industrial relations and trade unions, in *Africa in Wirtschaft und Gesellschaft im Industriezeitalter*, 4 vol. encyclopaedia issued by the Union Press, Stuttgart 1976.

Appendix

13   with Richard Sandbrook, Workers and progressive change in underdeveloped countries', 'Introduction to Part 1', 'Introduction to Part 2', 'Introduction to Part 3' and 'Conclusion', all in R. Sandbrook and R. Cohen (eds) *The development of an African working class: studies in class formation and action* (London: Longman, 1975) pp. 1–9, 11–20, 127–38, 193–206, 311–16.

12   'Editorial', for issue on 'The State in Africa', *Review of African Political Economy*, vol. 3, no. 5, Spring 1976, pp. 1–3.

11   'Marxism and Africa' Working Paper no. 2, Centre for Developing Area Studies, *McGill University*, August 1975.

10   with David Michael, 'The revolutionary potential of the African lumpenproletariat: a sceptical view', *Bulletin of the Institute of Development Studies*, vol. 5 nos 2–3, October 1973.

9   with Arnold Hughes, 'Towards the emergence of a Nigerian working class: the social identity of the Lagos labour force, 1897–1939', Occasional Paper Series D, no. 7, Faculty of Commerce and Social Science, *University of Birmingham*, November 1972, 61 pp.

8   'Ethnicity, social class and political power: with some reference to Nigeria', Occasional Paper Series B, no. 14, Faculty of Commerce and Social Science, *University of Birmingham*, February 1971, 24 pp.

7   'A "Greater South": or what might have happened in the Nigerian civil war', Occasional Paper Series C, no. 22, Faculty of Commerce and Social Science, *University of Birmingham*, February 1971, 30 pp.

6   'Nigeria's central trade union organisation: a study guide', *Journal of Modern African Studies*, vol. 9, no. 3, October 1971, pp. 456–8.

5   'Nigeria's "Labour Leader No. 1": notes for a biographical study of M. A. O. Imoudu', *Journal of the Historical Society of Nigeria*, vol. 5, no. 2, June 1970, pp. 303–8.

4   'The army and trade unions in Nigerian politics', *Civilisations*, vol. 19, no. 2, June 1969, pp. 226–30.

3   'Why trade union disunity?' *Nigerian Opinion*, vol. 4, nos 4–6, April/June 1968, pp. 333–6.

2   'Trade union dilemmas in the current situation', *Nigerian Opinion*, vol. 4, nos 2–3, February–March 1968.

1   'Pamphleteers on the Left', *Nigerian Opinion*, vol. 3, no. 12, January 1968.

PUBLICATIONS FORTHCOMING

'Islands, migration and imagination', in Anthology in celebration of Russell King, to be published by University of Sussex

A migrating mind: a memoir of eight universities (in preparation)

With Jason Cohen, 'Self-surveillance: you are Big Brother' (in preparation)

REVIEWS

Reviews have appeared in over 50 journals, namely:

Africa
African Affairs
African Business
African Economic History
Africana Journal
Anti-Apartheid News
British Journal of Sociology
Bulletin of Eastern Caribbean Affairs
Canadian Journal of African Studies
Canadian Review of Sociology & Anthropology
Capital & Class
Caribbean Contact
Caribbean Issues
Development & Change
Diaspora: a Journal of Transnational Studies
Ethnic & Racial Studies
History
Immigrants & Minorities
International Affairs
International Journal of African Historical Studies
International Journal of Comparative Race & Ethnic Studies
International Journal of Urban & Regional Research
International Review of Social History
Journal of African History
Journal of Commonwealth Political Studies
Journal of Developing Areas
Journal of Development Studies

Journal of Ethnic History
Journal of Global History
Journal of Historical Geography
Journal of International Development
Journal of Refugee Studies
Labor History
Labour History Review
Labour, Capital & Society
Newsletter of International Labour Studies
New Community
New Society
New West Indian Guide
Political Studies
Popular Music: a Yearbook
Quarterly Journal of Social Affairs
Review of African Political Economy
Science & Society
Sociology in Wales
Sunday Telegraph
The Sociological Review
Times Educational Supplement (regular 1974–77)
Times Higher Educational Supplement
Times Literary Supplement
Third World Book Review
Third World Planning Review
Third World Quarterly
Transactions of the Historical Society of Ghana
West European Politics
Work, Employment & Society